D1283281

COVERED CALL WRITING WITH EXCHANGE TRADED FUNDS (ETFs)

Double-Digit Returns
Diversification
Downside Protection

Paul D. Kadavy

 Arrow Publications

✳ ARROW PUBLICATIONS
P.O. Box 19464
Fountain Hills, Arizona 85269-9464
E-Mail: arrowpublications@cox.net

Manufactured in the United States of America
Library of Congress Control Number: 2002095257
ISBN 0-9715514-2-1

Although the author has extensively researched appropriate sources to ensure the accuracy and completeness of the information contained in this publication, the author and the publisher assume no responsibility for errors, inaccuracies, omissions, or any inconsistency herein.

This publication is designed to provide accurate and authoritative information in regard to the subject matter covered. It is sold with the understanding that neither the author nor the publisher is engaged in rendering legal, tax, accounting, investment, or other professional services. No such advice is intended or implied.

All securities named in this publication have been included purely for purposes of illustration. No recommendation to buy, sell, or hold such securities, or any securities, is intended. Readers should use their own judgment. If advice or other expert assistance is required, the services of a competent professional person should be sought.

Trademark notice: Product or corporate names may be trademarks or registered trademarks, and are used only for identification and explanation, without intent to infringe.

CONTENTS

PREFACE

The Exchange Traded Fund (ETF) is one of the most exciting and innovative products to come out of the securities industry in years. An ETF represents shares of ownership in portfolios of common stocks which are designed to generally correspond to the price and yield performance of their underlying portfolios of securities...either broad market, industry sector, regions, investment styles or international. ETFs give investors the opportunity to buy or sell an entire portfolio of stocks within a single security, as easily as buying or selling a share of stock. They offer ownership diversification through a wide range of investment opportunities with much greater flexibility than mutual funds.

Despite the attractiveness of this relatively new investment vehicle, investments in ETFs remain fundamentally investments in the stock market, which make them subject to the same opportunities and risks as the underlying stocks they contain. In other words, despite the inherent advantages of diversification, ease of trading and cost efficiency, the investment performance of ETFs, for better or for worse, will only mirror the same performance of the stocks that comprise them.

Many investment experts and economists have been making public statements about investor expectations for the long-term future. This includes, among many others, two exceptionally prominent individuals: Warren Buffett, Chairman of Berkshire Hathaway, often referred to as the "Oracle of Omaha" for the incredible investment success he has achieved over the past four decades, and John Templeton, mutual fund pioneer and founder of the Templeton mutual funds.

Unfortunately these experts are strongly suggesting that investors should not hope for anywhere near the level of investment returns from the stock market that they have come to expect over the past two decades. Buffett and Templeton believe that, at best, investors may realize from five-percent to seven-percent annual returns before taxes and inflation going forward. Thus, even with the advantages ETFs offer us, keeping our money and making it grow may become more difficult than it has been in the past for many years to come.

If this prediction from such highly qualified experts is close to accurate, new ideas will be needed if stock market investors are to have any hope of achieving double-digit returns in the future.

The program presented in this book is elegant in its simplicity and power-packed in its potential for the average investor. It involves two simple steps: (1) the use of Exchange Traded Funds as the investment vehicle of choice to obtain the requisite diversification needed by equity investors, and (2) the use of covered call option writing in conjunction with those Exchange Traded Funds to yield consistent double-digit returns on investment.

With ETFs both the novice and the seasoned investor can achieve portfolio diversification as well as focus (e.g., broad market, industry sectors, regions, investment styles, or international) without the need to develop personal expertise in financial analysis and stock selection techniques. It also means there is no need to devote large amounts of time to researching individual stocks.

By writing covered calls on the ETFs you own or acquire, consistent double-digit returns are possible in a market where total returns from capital appreciation and dividends alone may be far less, if the experts are correct in their beliefs.

COVERED CALL WRITING WITH EXCHANGE TRADED FUNDS (ETFs) is designed both for people who already have investment assets as well as those who are accumulating money on a regular basis. It is for those who want first to preserve it from the effects of inflation and also want to make it grow to support them and to add to their wealth while assuming an acceptable amount of risk commensurate with the return.

This book is believed to be the only title exclusively devoted to the subject of covered call option writing with Exchange Traded Funds. It presents the subject material in a manner easy for the reader to understand and with a personal investment program for implementation by the reader. Software templates for a personal computer using Microsoft® Excel are provided with the book to assist the user in formulating investment decisions on covered call writing opportunities, for tracking results and to assist with other financial planning decisions.

The purpose of this book is to serve as a hands-on, practical workbook for individuals who seek to achieve a consistent double-digit total return compounded annually, year after year, on the equity portion of their investment assets, represented by the ownership of ETFs. Given market expectations, it provides what may be one of the best opportunities to achieve double-digit investment returns in the future.

By writing (selling) call option contracts on ETFs, the investor receives current income from option premiums, in addition to any dividends on the stocks owned by the ETF, and a defined amount of capital appreciation potential on the ETF. This approach is more conservative than simply owning equity investments alone. It can provide more stable, predictable, and higher investment returns than equity ownership alone in a slower growth stock market with the diversification that could otherwise only be obtained by owning a large number of individual stocks. This approach provides the diversification that has long been the hallmark of mutual funds with the added advantage of providing significant additional income from option premiums. Covered calls can be written on ETFs, but not on mutual funds.

How important is it to earn consistent double-digit returns on our investable funds? Let's examine this by assuming that an investor has an initial investment of $100,000 in a Rollover IRA account. Therefore, there are no current taxes to pay on investment gains and income. The difference in the value of the account over many years is staggering when applying a range of compounded annual returns. Consider the implications if it were possible to achieve a fifteen-percent compounded annual return...one that would have been considered to be a minimum expectation in the 1990s:

Rate:	6%	15%
Year:		
10	$179,085	$404,556
20	$320,714	$1,636,654
30	$574,349	$6,621,177

After ten years the person who earns fifteen-percent compounded annually has investments valued at well over twice the amount of the person who earns six-percent. After twenty years, the fifteen-percent return creates value more than five times the six-percent return. And, for investors fortunate enough to have an even longer time horizon, after thirty years there is greater than an eleven-time difference. This clearly demonstrates the multiplier effect of not only earning a return on your principal, but also earning a return on your return...the magic of compounding. Albert Einstein called compounding "The most powerful principle I ever witnessed." Ben Franklin called it "The Eighth Wonder of the World." There doesn't seem to be any doubt that they were correct, given the magnitude of the figures above.

The program provided in this book to assist you in achieving double-digit compounded annual returns might be more conservative or more aggressive than your current investment approaches. Suffice it to say for now that the program involves more risk than placing your money in a bank, but less risk than simply being invested in the stock market.

We should never underestimate the ability of inflation to diminish our purchasing power over long periods of time. By achieving a double-digit annualized return, an investor could expect to outpace inflation many times over. Most people would be able to add considerably to their net worth each year or could produce extra income to cope with rising expenses and improve their overall standard of living.

This book is for those who believe that long-term inflation is always a risk to overcome, but are concerned that the stock market alone may not provide the returns that it has in the past. It is for those of you who hope to still achieve a double-digit annual return on your investments despite the predictions of a slower growth market. If you are willing to take some risk to accomplish this, but not as much risk as just being in the stock market alone, then this book is for you.

By using the tools in this book, you will have a viable means of working towards this worthwhile objective.

*   *   *   *   *

A brief word regarding the call option writing examples in this book. Hypothetical names have been used for individual ETFs (e.g., "AAA," "BBB," "JJJ" and so on). These do, however, represent actual option trading opportunities for real ETFs based upon data obtained at the time the examples were created. The names have been changed since information concerning real ETFs, such as price of securities and other information, becomes out of date immediately after the slice of time from which it was taken. Fortunately the principles applied in the examples remain valid.

The reader should be aware that brokerage commissions and other transaction costs have not been included in the investment calculations for the examples to simplify the subject matter presented. Such costs are discussed and would need to be considered in actual calculations. Provisions have been made to customize the software included with this book to fit the user's own commission schedule.

Prior to trading any option, an investor must receive a copy of *Characteristics and Risks of Standardized Options*. A copy may be obtained from the investor's broker or on the Internet at www.cboe.com.

Paul D. Kadavy

THE CASE FOR EXCHANGE TRADED FUNDS

Why would an investor or a prospective investor want to make use of Exchange Traded Funds (ETFs)? Traditionally investors have gravitated towards either mutual funds or individual stocks for their equity investments. Mutual funds have generally been the equity investment of choice for smaller investors, but many substantial investors indulge in them as well. The purchase of a small number of stocks in individual companies does not give the investor the diversification that can be achieved by owning shares in a mutual fund participating in a pool containing a large number of stocks.

Here are the key issues revolving around ETFs and some comparisons with ownership of mutual funds and individual stocks.

ETFs: A DEFINITION

What exactly are Exchange Traded Funds? They are a hybrid of listed corporate common stocks and mutual funds that are open-ended (continually offering new shares). ETFs are investment companies under the U.S. Tax Code and are regulated by the Securities and Exchange Commission. ETFs consist of a broad spectrum of securities (typically stocks, although bond ETFs also exist) designed to correspond to the price and yield performance of the underlying portfolio of securities. ETFs have been created to mirror many different themes: the **broad market** (Dow Jones, S&P 500, Wilshire 5000, Fortune 500); **industry sectors** (cyclical, retail, transportation, natural resources, oil service, basic materials, chemical, technology, financial, pharmaceutical, real estate); **size** (small cap, mid cap, large cap), **region** (Pacific, Europe), **investment style** (value, growth), and **international markets** (Australia, Austria, Belgium, Brazil, Canada, France, Germany, Hong Kong, Italy, Japan, Latin America, Malaysia, Mexico, Netherlands, Singapore, South Korea, Spain, Sweden, Switzerland, Taiwan, United Kingdom). Some ETFs utilize more than one theme, for example, broad market, international, small cap growth, large cap value, and so on.

The first commercially successful ETF, an S&P 500 index fund, began trading on the American Stock Exchange (AMEX) in January 1993. These shares are referred to as "Spiders," the name coming from Standard & Poors Depository Receipt (ticker symbol SPY).

HOW AN ETF IS CREATED

Unlike mutual finds, sponsors of ETFs do not sell ETF shares to investors for cash. An ETF consists of a portfolio of securities designed to closely mirror one or more of the themes stated above. The sponsor of an ETF, therefore, registers shares of the ETF and exchanges blocks of the ETF shares for the securities of the companies that make up the index on which the ETF is based. Another way of stating it is that the ETF manager delivers the newly created ETF shares to a market maker (broker-dealer) and receives back the entire portfolio of the individual underlying shares. For example, a sponsor creating an ETF based on the Dow Jones Industrial Average would issue ETF shares and exchange blocks of these shares for actual shares of the stocks comprising the Dow Jones Industrial Average. These ETF shares are then listed on one or more exchanges (all ETFs are listed on the American Stock Exchange) and are offered for sale to the public, typically by market makers or broker-dealers. These **"creation units"** are continuously developed based primarily on investor demand for them.

MANAGERS OF ETFs

The entity serving as manager of an ETF depends on the particular ETF product. For example, all of the ETF products within the group referred to as iShares are managed by Barclays Global Investors. All HOLDRs are managed by Merrill Lynch. "Spiders" (ticker symbol SPY), the largest ETF, is managed by State Street Bank and Trust Company and the Bank of New York. The Bank of New York also manages the NASDAQ-100 Investment Trust.

SUCCESS OF ETFs

As of mid 2002, over half of all of the volume of trades on the American Stock Exchange were ETF trades. As of the date of this writing, there are 123 ETFs listed on US exchanges, and the number is quickly growing. The collective value of these ETFs is approximately $100 billion. The largest ETF is the first one...the Spiders, with a value of approximately $30 billion. Second is the NASDAQ 100

Index Tracker (nicknamed "Cubes" because of its ticker symbol of QQQ), valued at about $20 billion.

FEATURES AND BENEFITS OF ETFs
VS. MUTUAL FUNDS AND INDIVIDUAL STOCKS

As mutual funds have long been an investment vehicle of choice for the public, it is important to compare ETFs with mutual funds to gain a better understanding of why ETFs have become so popular and why they are likely to increasingly become so in the future. While it would be premature to sound the death knell for mutual funds, an examination of the features and benefits of ETFs compared with mutual funds will speak for their attractiveness relative to each other in loud terms. A comparison of ETFs with individual stocks also demonstrates the appeal of ETFs.

DIVERSIFICATION

Exchange Traded Funds: A buyer of ETF shares gets instant exposure to a market or sector portfolio of stocks of his or her choice. By participating in a portfolio of a large number of stocks, an investor has ownership in a broader number of companies. This provides a degree of protection in the event that the price of one company in the index or sector should decline significantly.

Mutual Funds: Similar to ETFs in regard to diversification.

Individual Stocks: Unless you have time and know how to research and pick stocks and you can afford a portfolio of at least 10 and perhaps up to 20 stocks in different industries, you will not be diversified.

TRADING

Exchange Traded Funds: ETFs can be bought or sold as easily as a share of an individual stock. Shares may be bought and sold at any time during the trading day when markets are open. Pricing is continuously updated. Purchases and sales settle three days after the transaction is completed, as with individual stocks.

Mutual Funds: Typically only bought and sold at the end of the trading day after the market is closed, not intra-day, and are priced at net asset value. Purchases and sales settle immediately.

Individual Stocks: Same process as with ETFs.

AVAILABILITY OF LIMIT AND STOP ORDERS

Exchange Traded Funds: Both limit and stop orders are available, as with individual stocks.

Mutual Funds: Shares purchased directly from the offerer of the fund are bought and redeemed at the net asset value established by the fund at the end of the day. Therefore, limit and stop orders do not apply to such mutual funds.

Individual Stocks: Both limit and stop orders are available, as with ETFs.

DIVIDEND REINVESTMENT

Exchange Traded Funds: Each ETF establishes its own dividend policy. Some reinvest dividends immediately on an ongoing basis, while others reinvest quarterly. Some pay out cash to shareholders.

Mutual Funds: Dividends may be reinvested in shares at time of distribution by the fund (typically quarterly) or may be paid out to shareholders.

Individual Stocks: Companies that pay dividends make payment in cash on a quarterly basis. Some companies offer dividend reinvestment programs (so-called DRIPs) where a shareholder can elect to receive shares in lieu of cash dividends.

AVAILABILITY OF MARGIN

Exchange Traded Funds: ETFs may generally be purchased on margin under the same rules as for individual stocks.

Mutual Funds: Margin purchase of mutual funds is not permitted.

Individual Stocks: Many, but not all, individual stocks may generally be purchased on margin under the same rules as for ETFs.

SHORT SELLING

Exchange Traded Funds: All ETFs are eligible for short trading (the investor borrows shares from the broker in anticipation of declining market prices whereby the investor hopes the shares can be bought back at a lower price). Some ETFs are also exempt from the rule requiring shares to be sold short only when the last sale price is higher than the preceding sale (an "up tick").

Mutual Funds: Short selling is not available with mutual funds.

Individual Stocks: Short selling is available on most stocks.

TAX EFFICIENCY

Exchange Traded Funds: Ownership in an index results in much lower share turnover than most actively traded mutual funds. Investors do not experience the tax consequences that occur when stocks in a fund are frequently bought and sold. There are other factors that result in generally no tax consequences to ETF investors until they actually sell their shares.

Mutual Funds: Index based mutual funds also have lower share turnover. Managed funds with a high degree of purchase and sale activity generate significant tax consequences for shareholders.

Individual Stocks: Tax consequences are realized only when an individual stock is sold.

COST

Exchange Traded Funds: One of the most cost-effective means of an investment participation in a market or an index. Annual management fees typically range from 0.1% to 0.65%. ETFs generally charge fees similar to low cost, no-load index-based mutual funds. Brokerage commissions are also paid to buy and sell ETFs.

Mutual Funds: Some mutual funds charge a sales load fee of up to several percent in addition to the management fee that all mutual funds charge. For many mutual funds the management fee is considerably higher than for ETFs, with some professionally managed fund portfolios charging as much as 2% annually.

Individual Stocks: The cost of ownership is in the brokerage commissions to buy and sell the individual stocks. There are no annual management fees.

AVAILABILITY THROUGH BROKERAGES

Exchange Traded Funds: All ETFs can be purchased through any broker, whether full-service or discount.

Mutual Funds: Many mutual funds can only be purchased through a single company offering the fund. Some are available from a variety of brokers.

Individual Stocks: Individual stocks, as with ETFs, are available through any broker, whether full-service or discount.

AVAILABILITY OF STANDARDIZED OPTIONS (INCLUDING COVERED CALLS)

Exchange Traded Funds: There are a fast growing number of ETFs that offer options, which would allow the investor to write covered calls. This trend will no doubt continue in the future.

Mutual Funds: Options are not available on mutual funds.

Individual Stocks: Many individual stocks offer options, which would include the availability of covered call writing.

TIME REQUIREMENT

Exchange Traded Funds: ETFs are perfect for investors who do not have the time or lack the inclination to research and select individual stocks.

Mutual Funds: Mutual funds are also ideal for investors short on time or who do not have the desire to research and select individual stocks.

Individual Stocks: The most time consuming and potentially risky strategy for an investor.

INVESTMENT TRANSPARENCY

Exchange Traded Funds: With an ETF you always know what stocks comprise the portfolio in which you participate.

Mutual Funds: Almost all mutual funds report their actual holdings only twice per year, which means that fund investors seldom can determine exactly what they own.

Individual Stocks: Investors who purchase individual stocks always know what they own. The principal question is whether they understand what they own.

PRICE VOLATILITY

Exchange Traded Funds: Because they consist of the stocks from entire markets or sectors, ETFs have lower volatility than do individual securities.

Mutual Funds: Lower volatility than for individual securities is also inherent in mutual funds.

Individual Stocks: Volatility is stock specific, but individual stocks are inherently more volatile than portfolios consisting of many stocks.

SUITABILITY FOR DOLLAR COST AVERAGING

Exchange Traded Funds: For investors desiring to invest a small amount on a regular basis (dollar cost averaging) ETFs would not be the best choice. Each trade incurs a brokerage commission. For covered call writing, purchases of ETFs should always be in 100 share increments.

Mutual Funds: Mutual funds represent the best opportunity for investors making small, multiple purchases, as brokerage commissions would not come into play if the shares are purchased directly from the fund offerer.

Individual Stocks: The same comments regarding ETFs apply to individual stocks.

A strong case exists for the use of ETFs by both wealthy investors and those of lesser means who are building a portfolio. With the severe downturn in the equity markets, many mutual funds find themselves in a position of needing to liquidate fund assets in order to pay off customers redeeming their funds. This puts the mutual fund in a cash squeeze position that is not healthy for the fund or for the remaining customers. ETFs face no such challenge.

WARNINGS ABOUT
SLOW-GROWTH MARKETS

Despite the obvious advantages of Exchange Traded Funds, investments in ETFs, as with mutual funds and individual stocks, are still stock market investments. They should do well in rising markets, decline in falling markets, and will perform somewhere in between in a flat to slow-growth market environment.

Many of our most trusted financial experts are warning us that the generous stock market returns of the past should not be expected in the future. Warren Buffett, "The Oracle of Omaha," and arguably the most successful investor in modern times, has almost always been silent about his feelings toward the stock market in the past. In the last three years, he has been anything but silent. Just prior to the beginning of the huge NASDAQ decline, an article in *Fortune* magazine quoted statements Buffett made to some of his friends at a retreat, including the following:

> *Today, staring fixedly back at the road they just traveled, most investors have rosy expectations. I think it's very hard to come up with a persuasive case that equities will over the next 17 years perform anything like--anything like – they've performed in the past 17. If I had to pick the most probable return, from appreciation and dividends combined, that investors in aggregate--repeat, aggregate--would earn in a world of constant interest*

rates, 2% inflation, and those ever hurtful frictional costs, it would be 6%. If you strip out the inflation component from this nominal return (which you would need to do however inflation fluctuates), that's 4% in real terms. And if 4% is wrong, I believe that the percentage is just as likely to be less as more. [1]

He went on to say at the annual meeting of his company, Berkshire Hathaway, that investors should expect, "returns from equities that are dramatically less than most investors have either experienced in the past or expect in the future." [2] His associate, Vice Chairman Charlie Munger was also quoted as saying that six-percent to seven-percent would be a reasonable expectation of annual stock market growth for the next ten to twenty years. [3] One year later Buffett's statements in his annual report offered similar warnings. Buffett said, "Our restrained enthusiasm for these securities (referring to Berkshire Hathaway's stock holdings) is matched by decidedly lukewarm feelings about the prospects for stocks in general over the next decade or so." [4]

---

[1] Carol Loomis, "Mr. Buffett on the Stock Market," *Fortune* (Vol. 140, No. 10, Special Issue, November 22, 1999): 212.

[2] Comment made by Warren Buffett, Chairman of the Board of Berkshire Hathaway, Inc., at its annual shareholders meeting held April, 2001 in Omaha, Nebraska.

[3] Comment made by Charlie Munger, Vice Chairman of Berkshire Hathaway, Inc., at its annual shareholders meeting held April, 2001 in Omaha, Nebraska.

[4] "Chairman's Letter, "Berkshire Hathaway 2001 Annual Report: 15.

While it is possible that these experts could be wrong, history has certainly been on the side of those who have believed in Mr. Buffett.

WHY WILL MARKET GROWTH LIKELY BE SLOWER IN THE FUTURE?

There are many other financial experts who believe that stock market returns in the future will be significantly less than they have been in the past. They offer several themes to support their conclusions:

- Despite market corrections in the major averages...the Dow Jones Industrial Average, the Standard & Poors 500, and most especially the NASDAQ...stocks are still selling at heftier prices now than even a historical midpoint of a range of values for these averages.

- A bubble was created in the Internet and telecommunications sectors through unprecedented access by startup companies to the capital markets, resulting in unsustainable levels of capital spending. This has been unwinding for some time as the bubble burst. Many believe that such a bursting has long-term implications that will slow future economic growth and affect other industries as well.

- Corporate profits would have to grow at an abnormally high rate in the future as a percentage of Gross Domestic Product (national output) to support much higher stock prices. Since this is very unlikely, the relatively high level of current stock prices will increase more slowly as corporate earnings growth works to catch up and bring about   normalized stock price averages in the more distant future.

- Interest rates are now at lows not seen since the Kennedy Administration in the 1960s. Inflation is very low. Both of these factors certainly support relatively high stock prices. Yet to support significantly higher stock prices, both interest rates and inflation would need to decline even more. The problem is that there is almost no additional room for either to decline further.

These are the primary schools of thought regarding why stock prices are highly likely to grow at a slower pace in the future than they have in the past. Investors would be well served by watching these factors. For owners of stocks and ETFs, writing covered call options on them may be the best opportunity to achieve double-digit returns in this projected future.

Even though ETFs can provide many protective advantages to the investor, no equity investments, including ETFs, mutual funds and stocks of individual companies, can provide adequate protection or superior relative investment results in a declining market environment, a flat market, or even a slow-growth market.

THE BENEFITS AND RISKS
OF COVERED CALL WRITING

The principal problem investors face today is that there are no viable alternatives to the stock market for deploying investment resources to obtain double-digit returns. Let's consider the usual suspects...bonds, real estate, and tangible investments:

- **Bonds** – While there may be some additional capital appreciation potential in bonds should interest rates come down further, the coupon rate on bonds is already near 50-year lows due to the extremely low rate of inflation. Bonds have appreciated very substantially in recent years. They can provide an important fixed income component to a well-balanced investment portfolio; however, bonds do not outperform stocks over long periods of time.

- **Real estate** – Significant appreciation may potentially occur in well-selected real estate investments. Such investments are, however, generally quite illiquid. Investment advisors suggest only a small portion of investable assets should be placed into real estate investments.

- **Tangible investments, gold and other precious metals** – Such alternatives are very unlikely to outperform, as these assets rise in value primarily in a high inflationary environment and in times of ongoing crisis. Economists are generally predicting low inflation for the future. And even in today's tense international environment that may cause short-term swings, the long-term outlook would not point to investment outperformance of such assets.

A NEW PATH: COVERED CALL WRITING

With this as a backdrop, what is an investor to do? For those who are concerned that these projections are the likely future we will be facing, a new path is needed. As Yogi Berra supposedly said, "When you come to a fork in the road, take it." But which road can lead us to significantly above-average returns year after year without taking a path of undue risk?

This book will explore an investment opportunity widely known and used by savvy institutional investors...pension funds, insurance companies, trust departments and some mutual funds. It's little known and often misunderstood by individual investors.

With many experts projecting a long-term slow-growth stock market, or even no growth at all, a solid case can be made more strongly than ever that the time has come for the average investor, whether wealthy or currently accumulating wealth, to use a little known, but powerful investment strategy...covered call option writing on stocks that you own. And one of the many attractive aspects of this strategy is that it is becoming increasingly more available for use with Exchange Traded Funds.

Using standardized, exchange-traded options for covered call writing on ETFs, the combined return to the investor from potential capital appreciation, dividends and the additional income an investor receives from writing covered calls can result in double-digit yields...more predictably and conservatively than with common stocks alone. Covered call writing is a new subject for most individual investors and is misunderstood by many others. It is misunderstood, as many investors think of "options" and "calls" as being high risk, speculative strategies where large losses can be incurred. In reality, covered call writing is *more conservative* than investing in stocks or ETFs alone, can provide significant *protection in a down market*, and can be a key component for an investor to *achieve double-digit returns in a flat or slow-growth market*.

The program outlined in **COVERED CALL WRITING WITH EXCHANGE TRADED FUNDS (ETFs)**, a combination of prudent ownership of ETFs coupled with writing covered call options on them, provides what may be one of the best opportunities to achieve double-digit investment returns in the future.

Before beginning an in-depth discussion of ETF investments in conjunction with this potentially profitable investment strategy, a review of the benefits and risks of a covered call option writing program is in order:

THE BENEFITS OF COVERED CALL WRITING

1. Additional income - Writing covered call options can provide you with an ongoing stream of call writing income from your ETFs. This is particularly important at a time when most common stocks, mutual funds and ETFs either pay no dividends at all or they provide a very meager return on investment. The call writing income can also significantly enhance total returns in a flat or slower growth stock market.

2. **Income paid up front** - The income received from covered call writing is credited to your account the next day, creating immediate cash flow that can be reinvested to produce more income or can be withdrawn from your brokerage account for any use. Since the call writing income is paid up front, if the income is reinvested it can enhance the overall yield on the original investment.

3. **Predetermined return** – The immediate and annualized returns from call writing can all be evaluated prior to initiating the investment position. You will know what the call writing income will be and the maximum additional capital appreciation opportunity you will have for your ETFs.

4. **Risk reduction** - If an ETF declines in price, the call writing income you received helps to offset some, or all, of the decline in the ETF's value. Writing covered calls acts like an insurance policy offering some downside protection when an ETF declines in price.

5. **Cash dividends** – As a writer of covered calls, you will continue to be entitled to any cash dividends for as long as you own the ETF.

6. **Fungibility** – Exchange-listed options, as is true of individual stocks and ETFs, are fungible. That is, each listed option is interchangeable with any similar listed option. This enables investors to initiate and close out a position in the open market through their brokerage account. Fungible option contracts became available in 1973.

7. **Ease of trading** - Since options are actively traded on the open market, call option transactions can easily be conducted, similar to trading stocks and ETFs. With the assistance of this book, it is readily accomplished yourself with online or phone trading through a discount brokerage account or through a full-service broker.

8. **Diversification of ETFs for option writing** - There is a growing list of ETFs of all types that offer covered call writing. Unquestionably the number of ETFs that offer this will continue to become even more widely available in the future.

9. **Cash or margin account** - Covered call options may be written on ETFs either in a cash or a margin account (cash only for retirement accounts).

10. **Options listed in daily newspapers, brokerages, and online** - A table of actively traded listed options, their closing prices from the previous day, and other relevant data is available on a current basis in most daily newspapers. A detailed quote for any option is always available through online brokerage accounts. Many brokerages also have automated quotation systems for

customer use over the phone. Extensive online options quotations are also available through the Yahoo! Finance section on the Internet (www.yahoo.com) and other similar sources.

THE RISKS OF COVERED CALL WRITING

1. **Investing in the stock market** - Writing covered call options requires that the investor own stocks or Exchange Traded Funds, which are stock market investments that are subject to market risk. Writing covered calls, however, provides some downside protection in declining markets. Therefore, the investor in stocks or Exchange Traded Funds on which covered call options have been written is always better off if they decline in value than the investor who owns the same stocks or ETFs but does not write covered call options.

2. **Limited gains in a rising market** - An option writer's potential gain is limited to the amount of call writing income received plus any gain in the price of the underlying ETF from the time the option was written up to the dollar amount of the strike price (See Glossary. This term and related concepts are used in subsequent chapters). Depending on the strike price and the extent of a rise in the underlying ETF prior to the expiration date (see Glossary), in a rapidly rising market the option writer may not benefit from all of the rise in an ETF. While still profitable, an option writer faces the risk that it might have been better financially to have simply held the ETF and not written covered call options in a rapidly rising market.

3. **Unanticipated exercise of call options** – The holder (buyer) of a call option has the right, but not the obligation, to buy (exercise) the option writer's ETF at the strike price at any time through the expiration date. A writer can expect that his ETF will rarely be subject to exercise if the market price of the ETF is less than the strike price of the call option written. If, however, the market price rises above the strike price, it is possible that the holder could exercise the call option at any time, thus requiring the option writer to sell the underlying ETF at the strike price. Exercise of options generally occurs at the expiration date, and then usually only if the market price exceeds the strike price. On occasion, however, a holder will exercise an option prior to the expiration date. This is beneficial in some respects for the option writer, as the writer is paid the strike price early and can decide how to deploy the funds immediately instead of having to wait until the expiration date.

4. **Potential lack of option market liquidity** – Options generally trade in much smaller quantities than common stock or ETF shares. Options for some ETFs are very actively traded. For other ETFs there are usually fewer option contracts traded. This may cause the bid and ask price spread to widen significantly. For this reason, investors are encouraged to always place limit orders (see Glossary) with their brokers on option trades instead of market orders to eliminate the risk of an order being filled at a different price than what a current quote might indicate.

5. **Possibility of a decrease in option premiums** – The price of a covered call writing option premium (see Glossary) is determined by market forces and mathematical models. During periods of market volatility, option premiums tend to be greater than during periods of stable markets. It is not possible to predict future volatility. Should markets become less volatile, or should markets be less attractive to investors in the future, it is possible that option premiums may not be as large as they have been in the past. Such an occurrence would tend to make the returns on covered call writing less attractive than they have been during periods of larger option premiums.

6. **Commissions on option trades** – The commissions charged by full-service brokers and discount brokers vary significantly. It is important to the investor to find a brokerage, whether discount or full-service, where commission costs can be reasonably managed.

If any of the above is confusing at this point, do not lose heart. The following chapters outline in detail the particular usages of ETFs in a covered call writing program. Therein a full understanding of the benefits and risks of covered call writing will be had.

SOME BACKGROUND INFORMATION ON COVERED CALL WRITING

This book will give you the theoretical and practical tools necessary to develop an investment discipline that will help you achieve double-digit investment returns on your investments through "**covered call option writing**" on your ETFs.

What comes to mind with the words "**call**" or "**option**"? Many investors would say they think of high risk, where a person might lose their entire investment. Actually, that can be very true for some types of option investors. But that has NOTHING to do with the investment program provided in this book. Quite the opposite. In fact, the covered call option writing program outlined here can take big losses by others and turn them into your profits! The investment *for them may be high risk*, but *your investment is very conservative* as you will soon see.

What is meant by the term "**covered**"? This simply means that you own shares of the ETF that stands behind the options...that you have the ETF to deliver if it is sold. There is also such a thing as "**uncovered.**" You won't have anything to do with that, though. It's an extremely high-risk strategy. It means you are writing calls on shares that you don't own. Suffice it to say that there is the potential for unlimited losses, which makes it the mirror image of our strategy.

The term **"writing"** when used in conjunction with covered calls simply means selling...you are selling calls on ETFs you own.

THE KEY DISCUSSION TOPICS

Our program will revolve around these subjects: what covered call options are and how they work; how and where they are traded; how to decide which covered calls to write; how to use an Excel spreadsheet template included with this book to assist you in those decisions; how to select and use a broker to execute your transactions; how to evaluate your success in meeting your investment program goals; and some information on tax matters.

But first we need to introduce some additional new terms and define them.

The program involves the use of an investment referred to as an **"option contract,"** which defines the rights and obligations of the parties involved. There are only three actions investors need to take with this program to achieve their investment objectives using covered call option contracts:

- Select appropriate ETFs on which call options can be written.
- Select the specific covered call option contracts to be written.
- Initiate the trades.

This cycle is then repeated over and over.

This program requires that you already have some knowledge of the equity markets and either know what ETFs you want to own or have the ability to do some research and make those decisions. If you feel you are in need of an education or a refresher on the markets and ETFs, please refer to the appropriate suggested readings and Internet Web sites listed in the Appendix.

This program, covered call option writing, has been available for decades. Nobody talks much about it though, and most people aren't involved in it. But it is widely accepted by many knowledgeable individual and **"institutional investors"** (mutual funds, bank trust departments, insurance companies, brokerage firms, pension funds...that sort of very large investor). Any reputable full-service or discount brokerage firm can verify the validity and usefulness of writing covered calls on ETFs. They provide brokerage services not only for stocks and ETFs, but also for options as part of what they do for their customers.

COVERED CALL WRITING IN A NUTSHELL

Here is a highly abridged version of what this is all about. You will not be *buying* call options, which is a potentially high-risk strategy, but rather you will be *selling* call options on ETFs you already own or will acquire, also known as *writing*. This is a very conservative, yet potentially lucrative option investing strategy. When you sell an option on an ETF that you own you are selling a window of time in which the buyer has the right to buy your ETF at a set price. The buyer is hoping that the price of your ETF is going to go up significantly during this window of time that the option is active...in other words, before the option expires. When you sell an option on your ETF, you are performing a transaction known as "writing a covered call," or, more simply "writing calls," or just "call writing." By writing covered calls, you can lower the downside risk on your investment, you can predict with greater accuracy how much money you will make, and you can help stabilize your profits. Selling the right to buy your ETF to others gives you the ability to make consistent and significant returns on your investments, and the buyer immediately pays you money to do this.

That's a mouthful, but it's the essence of it. You may not understand much about it now, but by the time some definitions, examples and calculations are reviewed, you will become much more comfortable with how it works. It will become second nature to you and you'll be ready to start making money with the program.

Before advancing to that level, however, it is time to answer some questions and also introduce additional important terms and provide their definitions. These terms will be used frequently going forward. (Note: An alphabetical listing of the terms appearing in bold type throughout this book and their definitions is located in the Glossary.)

WHAT IS AN OPTION?

The *buyer* of an option has the right, but not the obligation, to buy or sell an ETF for a specified price on or before a specific date. A "**call**" is the right to *buy* the ETF...like calling it away from you...while a "**put**" is the right of an ETF owner to *sell* the ETF...like putting it into your hands. The investor who purchases an option, whether it is a call or a put, is the option buyer. Conversely, the person who initiates a transaction by selling a call is the call option *seller* or *writer*. The buyer of the option is *not* obligated to buy the ETF, but the seller *is* obligated to sell if the buyer decides to "**exercise**" his right of purchase under the option. When the buyer of a call exercises the option, the seller's ETF shares are said to be "**assigned**," meaning they will be sold. In the case of our investment program, you will *always* be the seller of options. And with this program you will only be dealing with calls, not puts. The subject of puts will not be brought up again.

WHERE ARE COVERED CALL OPTIONS TRADED?

Option contracts are considered to be securities. As such, they are bought and sold through a brokerage firm. Either a full-service brokerage or a discount brokerage can be used, although option trades through a discount broker are usually much less expensive. Option contracts trade on U.S. securities exchanges, such as the Chicago Board Options Exchange (CBOE), the American Stock Exchange (ASE), the Philadelphia Stock Exchange (PHLX) and the Pacific Stock Exchange (PSE). The contracts traded on all of the exchanges are issued, guaranteed and cleared, that is to say settled or finalized, by the "**Options Clearing Corporation (OCC)**." The OCC is a registered clearing corporation with the "**Securities & Exchange Commission (SEC)**." It's not necessary to understand any more than that, except that this provides you with needed protection to assure your transactions fit certain common standards and that they all are handled through an independent and unbiased third party.

HOW IS MONEY MADE
WRITING COVERED CALLS?

An investor can make money three ways. First, you are always paid cash, called a "**premium,**" for giving someone the right to buy your ETF shares from you at a specific price, which is called the "**strike price,**" on or before the "**expiration date**" when the option expires. You get to keep the premium money whether or not the shares are actually bought from you later. There are typically a variety of strike prices available, some of which will usually be below the current market price of the ETF and some of which will be above it. There are also a variety of option expiration dates available that extend out as short as the current and the next month to about three years for options on some ETFs. These very long-term options, whose expirations range from one to about three years, are referred to as "**LEAPS,**" which stands for "Long-Term Equity Anticipation Securities." They are traded through your broker the same as other options.

Second, it should be standard practice under this program that the strike price on the options you write be *higher* than the current market value of the ETF on which you are writing options. This is referred to as being "**out-of-the-money.**" For example, if the current price of the ETF on which you are writing options is $28 and you write an option with a $30 strike price, the option is said to be out-of-the-money by $2. This means, in addition to the premium income, you can also potentially receive additional **"capital appreciation."** That's the difference between the price of an ETF when a call option is written and the strike price of the call option. Your ETF would likely be sold, that is to say "called away from you," or "assigned," if the price of the ETF is above $30 per share on the option expiration date. You would get to keep your option premium, plus your ETF would be called away at $30 per share, which is $2 per share greater than it was when you wrote the call option.

Third, if your ETFs pay dividends, you have that source of income as well. You are the owner of the ETF during the option period, so any dividends that are declared with an ex-dividend date taking place when you own the ETF means the dividends belong to you...and that obviously enhances your yield as you combine it with the option writing income and any capital appreciation to calculate your total yield.

If you were to write an option with a strike price *lower* than the current price of the ETF, the option is said to be **"in-the-money."** For example, if the current price of the ETF is $32 and you write an option with a $30 strike price, the option is said to be in-the-money by $2. As we will see later, you would receive a higher premium by writing an in-the-money option when compared to an out-of-the-money option, but you could actually incur a loss on your ETF compared with its price on the date you wrote the option if you write the in-the-money option. If the price in this example remained the same, you would receive only $30 per share for an ETF that was worth $32 at the time you wrote the option, or a loss of $2 per share from the market price at the time the option was written. You would rarely, if ever, want to do this.

Finally, when the market price of an ETF is exactly the same as the strike price of an option, the option is said to be "at-the-money." An example of this would be if you were interested in a call option with a strike price of $25 and the "underlying ETF," that is to say the ETF you own on which you would be writing the call options, was selling at exactly $25 per share.

All of this will be simplified shortly with more detailed examples.

WHAT IS A STRIKE PRICE AND HOW ARE THEY DETERMINED?

A strike price is the actual price at which the buyer of the option has the right to purchase the ETF covered by the option. Typically each ETF that trades options offers at least several different strike prices for each expiration date. Strike prices are established when the underlying ETF either advances or declines to a certain price level and trades consistently around that level. If, for example, XYZ ETF was trading at $49, hit a price of $50 and traded consistently at this level, a new and higher strike price may be added by the exchange where the option is traded. Volatile ETFs that trade in a broader range of prices would have more strike prices available for selection, some of which would be above the current market price for the ETF and some of which would be below. Strike prices are typically established in $5 increments, although $2 ½ increments are sometimes used, particularly when the ETF price is lower. The notable exception to this is the Nasdaq-100 Index Tracking Stock (QQQ). This popular ETF trades in huge volume and so do the call contracts associated with it. Therefore, strike prices have been set in $1 increments both above and below the current market price.

WHEN DOES THE CALL WRITER RECEIVE THE PREMIUM INCOME MONEY?

Once you've written a call the cash premium is deposited into your brokerage account THE NEXT BUSINESS DAY, even though you have not earned it yet. That's one of the many attractive benefits of this program mentioned earlier. No waiting! The premium is paid to you in cash...and, it is yours to use or invest *now* to earn even more money for yourself. Obviously this represents a big difference from waiting around for your interest to be paid on a bank CD or bond.

WHAT IS THE EXPIRATION DATE?

The expiration date is the last day on which an option may be exercised by the option buyer. This date is officially the Saturday immediately following the third Friday of the expiration month. If Friday is a holiday, the last trading day will be the preceding Thursday.

WHAT IF THE ETF A CALL IS WRITTEN ON DROPS SIGNIFICANTLY IN PRICE?

Obviously a decline in an ETF's price can happen to anyone in a bad market. If it didn't, everyone in the world would invest everything they have in ETFs and the stock market. When you write call options on an ETF and the ETF price goes down, the price of the options go down too. You could then buy the options back at a lower price than you sold them for and realize a profit on the difference. Or you can wait until expiration when the calls would be worthless. Then you've realized the entire premium income as gain. That's how the downside protection comes into play when you write covered calls.

Just like ETFs, call options are traded continuously on the exchanges. This is because option contracts, like ETFs, are "fungible" assets. That means you can buy and sell the same option contract at any time prior to expiration, because the contracts are identical and are interchangeable with other investors on the exchanges where they are traded.

The bid and ask prices of the option change too, even from minute to minute, as the price of the underlying ETF changes and as the time to expiration becomes shorter so there is less time remaining. Strategies for a declining ETF price will be discussed in more detail later. Just keep in mind that if an ETF declines you will *always* be better off if you have written call options on it than if you just owned the ETF by itself, because the premium you receive gives you some "downside protection."

WHAT IF THE ETF A CALL IS WRITTEN ON SHOOTS WAY UP IN PRICE?

There is a downside. A declining ETF price should not be considered a downside to writing covered calls, because the premium you receive gives you some protection against a declining ETF price. In other words, you are better off than if you just owned the ETF alone. The downside for the option writer occurs when the ETF price shoots up way above your strike price plus the option premium received and is in that position on the expiration date. In such a case, the option writer would have been better off just owning the ETF and not writing the options.

But, while the option writer may have lost in the sense that the call writing transaction didn't capture the entire rise in the ETF, by receiving the premium income plus the gain up to the strike price, the investor has obtained the maximum objective sought when the calls were initially written. That's a downside with an upside!

If your ETF goes way up, there are some choices, which will be covered in more detail. You can wait to see if your ETF gets called away from you at expiration. Another choice is to buy back the call at what could be a higher price than you initially sold it for. By doing this you release your obligation to sell the ETF, but that strategy is rarely recommended, as will be discussed later.

WHAT IF THE ETF SHARES DON'T GET CALLED AWAY AT EXPIRATION?

It varies, but about eighty-percent of the time options written out-of-the-money expire without being exercised. If the expiration date comes and goes and your ETF was not called away, this means you still own the ETF and you have earned the premium. You can then sell the ETF at its current market value, just continue to hold the ETF, or write another call and collect another premium.

UNDER WHAT CIRCUMSTANCES WILL AN ETF LIKELY BE CALLED AWAY?

You can anticipate having your ETF called away, referred to as being "assigned," any time your option becomes in-the-money. This almost always occurs at expiration if the market price of the ETF is greater than the strike price, although it could possibly happen at any time during the term of the option contract if the buyer of the option wanted to exercise the right earlier.

IF THE CALLS I WRITE EXPIRE WITHOUT BEING EXERCISED AND I GET TO KEEP ALL OF THE PREMIUM INCOME, DO I HAVE TO PAY A COMMISSION AT EXPIRATION?

No. As a writer of call options, the only time you pay an option commission is when you initiate the transaction or close out your position by buying it back. Closing it out is almost never recommended. If the option expires worthless, as a call writer you keep the entire option premium and pay no additional commission at expiration.

THE WORLD OF
EXCHANGE TRADED FUNDS

The number of Exchange Traded Funds offered to the public for investment has grown exponentially in just the past two years. Even more impressive is the growth in the number of these ETFs on which options are offered. As of the date of this printing, there are 118 Exchange Traded Funds currently available to the investing public. Of these, 49 offer the ability to write covered calls. Both categories should continue to grow significantly as the advantages of ETFs become more and more apparent to the investing public and interest in options on them grows.

Beginning on the next page is a list of all ETFs currently traded, sorted by ticker symbol, along with the investment category and whether options are currently offered.

All ETFs have been included in this list, as many of them that do not currently offer options may well do so in the future. Investors finding funds that interest them, but that do not currently offer options, should check back from time to time to see if options are subsequently offered. New ETFs available in the future can be found on the Internet by going to either www.amex.com or www.nasdaq.com and clicking on the section listing ETFs. Interested investors are also able to view a list of the top holdings for some of these ETFs, compare investment performance and request a prospectus online. For investors who do not have Internet access themselves, many public libraries offer this service at no charge.

ETF NAME	SYMBOL	CATEGORY	OPTIONS OFFERED?
Merrill Lynch Biotech HOLDRS	BBH	SECTOR	YES
Merrill Lynch Broadband HOLDRS	BDH	SECTOR	YES
Merrill Lynch B2B Internet HOLDRS	BHH	SECTOR	YES
streetTRACKS D.J. Global Titans Index Fund	DGT	BROAD BASED	NO
DIAMONDS Trust Series I	DIA	BROAD BASED	YES
streetTRACKS D.J. U.S. Small Cap Growth Index Fund	DSG	BROAD BASED	NO
streetTRACKS D.J. U.S. Small Cap Value Index Fund	DSV	BROAD BASED	NO
iShares MSCI - EAFE	EFA	INTERNATIONAL	NO
Merrill Lynch Europe 2001 HOLDRS	EKH	INTERNATIONAL	YES
streetTRACKS D.J. U.S. Large Cap Growth Index Fund	ELG	BROAD BASED	NO
streetTRACKS D.J. U.S. Large Cap Value Index Fund	ELV	BROAD BASED	NO
iShares MSCI Pacific Ex-Japan Index Fund	EPP	INTERNATIONAL	NO
*iShares MSCI - Australia	EWA	INTERNATIONAL	NO
iShares MSCI - Canada	EWC	INTERNATIONAL	NO
iShares MSCI - Sweden	EWD	INTERNATIONAL	NO
iShares MSCI - Germany	EWG	INTERNATIONAL	NO
iShares MSCI - Hong Kong	EWH	INTERNATIONAL	NO
iShares MSCI - Italy	EWI	INTERNATIONAL	NO
iShares MSCI - Japan	EWJ	INTERNATIONAL	NO
iShares MSCI - Belgium	EWK	INTERNATIONAL	NO
iShares MSCI - Switzerland	EWL	INTERNATIONAL	NO
iShares MSCI - Malaysia (Free)	EWM	INTERNATIONAL	NO
iShares MSCI - Netherlands	EWN	INTERNATIONAL	NO
iShares MSCI - Austria	EWO	INTERNATIONAL	NO
iShares MSCI - Spain	EWP	INTERNATIONAL	NO
iShares MSCI - France	EWQ	INTERNATIONAL	NO
iShares MSCI - Singapore (Free)	EWS	INTERNATIONAL	NO
iShares MSCI - Taiwan	EWT	INTERNATIONAL	NO
iShares MSCI - United Kingdom	EWU	INTERNATIONAL	NO
iShares MSCI - Mexico (Free)	EWW	INTERNATIONAL	NO
iShares MSCI - South Korea	EWY	INTERNATIONAL	NO
iShares MSCI - Brazil	EWZ	INTERNATIONAL	NO
iShares MSCI - European Monitary Union Index Fund	EZU	INTERNATIONAL	NO
FORTUNE e-50 Index Tracking Stock	FEF	SECTOR	YES
FORTUNE 500 Index Tracking Stock	FFF	BROAD BASED	YES
Merrill Lynch Internet HOLDRS	HHH	SECTOR	YES
Merrill Lynch Internet Architecture HOLDRS	IAH	SECTOR	YES
iShares NASDAQ Biotechnology Index Fund	IBB	SECTOR	YES
iShares Cohen & Steers Realty Majors Index Fund	ICF	SECTOR	NO
iShares Dow Jones U.S. Utilities Sector Index Fund	IDU	SECTOR	NO
iShares S&P Europe 350	IEV	INTERNATIONAL	NO
iShares Goldman Sachs Natural Resources Index Fund	IGE	SECTOR	NO
iShares Goldman Sachs Technology Index Fund	IGM	SECTOR	NO
iShares Goldman Sachs Network Index Fund	IGN	SECTOR	NO

iShares Goldman Sachs Software Index Fund	IGV	SECTOR	NO
iShares Goldman Sachs Semiconductor Index Fund	IGW	SECTOR	YES
Merrill Lynch Internet Infrastructure HOLDRS	IIH	SECTOR	YES
iShares S&P MidCap 400 Index Fund	IJH	BROAD BASED	YES
iShares S&P MidCap 400/BARRA Value	IJJ	BROAD BASED	YES
iShares S&P MidCap 400/BARRA Growth	IJK	BROAD BASED	YES
iShares S&P SmallCap 600 Index Fund	IJR	BROAD BASED	YES
iShares Small Cap 600/BARRA Value Index Fund	IJS	BROAD BASED	NO
iShares Small Cap 600/BARRA Growth Index Fund	IJT	BROAD BASED	NO
iShares S&P TSE 60 Index Fund	IKC	INTERNATIONAL	NO
iShares S&P Latin America 40 Index Fund	ILF	INTERNATIONAL	NO
iShares S&P Global 100 Index Fund	IOO	INTERNATIONAL	NO
iShares S&P TOPIX 150 Index Fund	ITF	INTERNATIONAL	NO
iShares S&P 500/BARRA Value Index Fund	IVE	BROAD BASED	NO
iShares S&P 500 Index Fund	IVV	BROAD BASED	NO
iShares S&P 500/BARRA Growth Index Fund	IVW	BROAD BASED	NO
iShares Russell 1000 Index Fund	IWB	BROAD BASED	YES
iShares Russell 1000 Value Index Fund	IWD	BROAD BASED	YES
iShares Russell 1000 Growth Index Fund	IWF	BROAD BASED	YES
iShares Russell 2000 Index Fund	IWM	BROAD BASED	YES
iShares Russell 2000 Value Index Fund	IWN	BROAD BASED	YES
iShares Russell 2000 Growth Index Fund	IWO	BROAD BASED	YES
iShares Russell MidCap Growth Index Fund	IWP	BROAD BASED	NO
iShares Russell MidCap Index Fund	IWR	BROAD BASED	NO
iShares Russell MidCap Value Index Fund	IWS	BROAD BASED	NO
iShares Russell 3000 Index Fund	IWV	BROAD BASED	YES
iShares Russell 3000 Value Index Fund	IWW	BROAD BASED	NO
iShares Russell 3000 Growth Index Fund	IWZ	BROAD BASED	NO
iShares S&P Global Energy Index Fund	IXC	SECTOR	NO
iShares S&P Global Financial Index Fund	IXG	SECTOR	NO
iShares S&P Global Healthcare Index Fund	IXJ	SECTOR	NO
iShares S&P Global Info Technology Index Fund	IXN	SECTOR	NO
iShares S&P Global Telecommunications Index Fund	IXP	SECTOR	NO
iShares D.J. U.S. Consumer Cyclical Sector Index Fund	IYC	SECTOR	NO
iShares D.J. U.S. Chemicals Index Fund	IYD	SECTOR	NO
iShares D.J. U.S. Energy Sector Index Fund	IYE	SECTOR	YES
iShares D.J. U.S. Financial Sector Index Fund	IYF	SECTOR	YES
iShares D.J. U.S. Financial Services Sector Index Fund	IYG	SECTOR	NO
iShares D.J. U.S. Healthcare Sector Index Fund	IYH	SECTOR	YES
iShares D.J. U.S. Industrial Sector Index Fund	IYJ	SECTOR	NO
iShares D.J. U.S. Cons. Non-Cyclical Sector Index Fund	IYK	SECTOR	NO
iShares D.J. U.S. Basic Materials Sector Index Fund	IYM	SECTOR	NO
iShares D.J. U.S. Real Estate Index Fund	IYR	SECTOR	NO
iShares D.J. U.S. Internet Index Fund	IYV	SECTOR	NO
iShares D.J. U.S. Technology Sector Index Fund	IYW	SECTOR	YES
iShares D.J. U.S. Total Market Index Fund	IYY	BROAD BASED	NO
iShares D.J. U.S. Telecom. Sector Index Fund	IYZ	SECTOR	YES
MidCap SPDR Trust Series I	MDY	BROAD BASED	YES
streetTRACKS Morgan Stanley Internet Index Fund	MII	SECTOR	NO
Merrill Lynch Market 2000+ HOLDRS	MKH	BROAD BASED	YES
streetTRACKS Morgan Stanley Technology Index Fund	MTK	SECTOR	NO
Merrill Lynch Market Oil Service HOLDRS	OIH	SECTOR	YES

Merrill Lynch Pharmaceutical HOLDRS	PPH	SECTOR	YES
Nasdaq-100 Index Tracking Stock	QQQ	BROAD BASED	YES
Merrill Lynch Regional Bank HOLDRS	RKH	SECTOR	YES
Merrill Lynch Retail HOLDRS	RTH	SECTOR	YES
streetTRACKS Wilshire REIT Index Fund	RWR	SECTOR	NO
Merrill Lynch Semiconductor HOLDRS	SMH	SECTOR	YES
SPDR Trust Series I	SPY	BROAD BASED	NO
Merrill Lynch Software HOLDRS	SWH	SECTOR	YES
Merrill Lynch Telecom HOLDRS	TTH	SECTOR	YES
Merrill Lynch Utilities HOLDRS	UTH	SECTOR	YES
Vanguard Total Stock Market VIPERs	VTI	BROAD BASED	YES
Vanguard Extended Market VIPERs	VXF	BROAD BASED	NO
Merrill Lynch Wireless HOLDRS	WMH	SECTOR	YES
Select Sector SPDR Fund - Basic Industries	XLB	SECTOR	YES
Select Sector SPDR Fund - Energy Select Sector	XLE	SECTOR	YES
Select Sector SPDR Fund - Financial	XLF	SECTOR	YES
Select Sector SPDR Fund - Industrial	XLI	SECTOR	YES
Select Sector SPDR Fund - Technology	XLK	SECTOR	YES
Select Sector SPDR Fund - Consumer Staples	XLP	SECTOR	YES
Select Sector SPDR Fund - Utilities	XLU	SECTOR	YES
Select Sector SPDR Fund - Consumer Services	XLV	SECTOR	YES
Select Sector SPDR Fund - Cyclical/Transportation	XLY	SECTOR	NO

Note: D.J. = Dow Jones

Of the ETFs that offer options, the list below, again sorted by ticker symbol, delineates the high and low daily share trading volume in the past year, and a ranking of the option choices and volume that will be of value to you as the technical aspects of covered call writing opportunities are discussed in future chapters.

SYMBOL	CATEGORY	ONE YEAR HIGH VOLUME SHS/DAY	ONE YEAR LOW VOLUME SHS/DAY	OPTION CHOICES	OPTION VOLUME
BBH	SECTOR	4,411,700	271,300	GOOD	GOOD
BDH	SECTOR	966,800	11,400	GOOD	POOR
BHH	SECTOR	621,600	22,400	POOR	POOR
DIA	BROAD BASED	24,678,000	869,600	EXCELLENT	GOOD
EKH	INTERNATIONAL	40,200	200	GOOD	POOR
FEF	SECTOR	32,900	100	FAIR	POOR
FFF	BROAD BASED	119,600	2,100	FAIR	FAIR
HHH	SECTOR	925,500	12,400	EXCELLENT	GOOD
IAH	SECTOR	1,075,500	4,500	FAIR	FAIR

IBB	SECTOR	2,080,400	41,200	GOOD	FAIR
IGW	SECTOR	634,200	1,300	POOR	POOR
IIH	SECTOR	3,281,900	7,200	POOR	POOR
IJH	BROAD BASED	301,000	15,300	GOOD	POOR
IJJ	BROAD BASED	429,900	7,500	GOOD	POOR
IJK	BROAD BASED	562,700	5,800	GOOD	POOR
IJR	BROAD BASED	870,500	39,100	GOOD	POOR
IWB	BROAD BASED	1,287,500	35,900	FAIR	GOOD
IWD	BROAD BASED	2,706,700	32,800	GOOD	FAIR
IWF	BROAD BASED	1,318,100	45,200	GOOD	FAIR
IWM	BROAD BASED	4,697,100	112,300	GOOD	GOOD
IWN	BROAD BASED	1,195,700	26,800	FAIR	GOOD
IWO	BROAD BASED	1,648,400	42,100	FAIR	GOOD
IWV	BROAD BASED	2,022,700	12,100	GOOD	POOR
IYE	SECTOR	211,600	3,600	POOR	POOR
IYF	SECTOR	255,800	1,300	FAIR	POOR
IYH	SECTOR	460,100	13,300	POOR	POOR
IYW	SECTOR	332,700	10,000	FAIR	GOOD
IYZ	SECTOR	700,900	6,000	FAIR	FAIR
MDY	BROAD BASED	5,431,900	567,800	EXCELLENT	GOOD
MKH	BROAD BASED	289,300	4,500	GOOD	FAIR
OIH	SECTOR	3,691,300	384,800	GOOD	GOOD
PPH	SECTOR	2,471,300	55,500	GOOD	GOOD
QQQ	BROAD BASED	98,829,300	4,809,900	EXCELLENT	EXCELLENT
RKH	SECTOR	1,126,100	17,800	GOOD	FAIR
RTH	SECTOR	1,829,700	40,300	FAIR	FAIR
SMH	SECTOR	13,179,200	1,958,100	GOOD	EXCELLENT
SWH	SECTOR	1,505,700	44,300	FAIR	FAIR
TTH	SECTOR	1,639,500	5,500	FAIR	FAIR
UTH	SECTOR	601,700	9,200	FAIR	FAIR
VTI	BROAD BASED	1,573,800	29,700	FAIR	FAIR
WMH	SECTOR	297,400	2,200	FAIR	FAIR
XLB	SECTOR	3,685,000	20,000	FAIR	POOR
XLE	SECTOR	5,281,200	61,800	FAIR	FAIR
XLF	SECTOR	11,048,700	83,800	FAIR	FAIR
XLI	SECTOR	2,663,200	18,900	FAIR	POOR
XLK	SECTOR	4,121,000	188,900	GOOD	GOOD
XLP	SECTOR	3,059,000	28,700	FAIR	POOR
XLU	SECTOR	665,200	14,300	FAIR	POOR
XLV	SECTOR	1,036,000	15,300	FAIR	POOR

You will note that for each of the ETFs offering options in this list, a classification has been given to indicate the breadth of "option choices" and "option volume." Each is rated EXCELLENT, GOOD, FAIR, or POOR. While any ETFs from this list may be effectively used for covered call writing, these classifications may be of assistance to you for several purposes. The "option choices" category refers to the number of different strike prices and expiration dates available to the call writer. Thus, those that are ranked EXCELLENT (e.g., QQQ) offer the greatest number of strike prices and expiration dates for options and those ranked POOR (e.g., IYH) offer the fewest. While an investor should not necessarily avoid an ETF with a ranking of POOR in the "option choices" category, it simply means that an owner of these ETFs will have a much harder time finding an appropriate strike price or expiration date to choose from. You might be forced into writing calls at a strike price or an expiration date that does not suit your personal needs from the standpoint of expiration date diversification or a strike price that does not coincide well with your outlook for the ETF or the market in general just because there are not adequate enough choices available to you. As you develop a target list of ETFs to buy now and in the future, you may wish to do more in-depth research by examining the breadth of strike prices and expiration dates available for ETFs on your list. (See Chapter 9 on brokerage accounts for more information).

The category of "option volume" refers to the daily volume of call contracts that are trading for each ETF. It also gives consideration to the **"open interest"** volume, which is the total number of call contracts that are in existence at a particular time. For options that are ranked EXCELLENT (e.g., SMH) the volume is the highest. Conversely, those ranked POOR (e.g., IGW) the volume is the lowest. The volume is a measure of the liquidity of the call contract and lets you know how easily the contract can be bought or sold. It is usually going to be more difficult to trade an option that has little volume than one that has high volume, both from the standpoint of speed and also possibly pricing. Few trades usually means that the spread between the bid and ask price is wider, which makes it more difficult to get orders filled at an acceptable price.

Contracts such as the QQQ are extremely attractive from the standpoint of liquidity and due to the broad number of strike prices and expiration dates offered. They are easy to trade, and orders get filled quickly. Contracts that are not widely followed and traded are the opposite. Many of these may become more actively traded in the future and may offer a wider range of strike prices and expiration dates. In the meantime, an investor who buys an ETF with a lower ranking in either the "option choices" or the "option volume" category should be very sure that the ETF is the most suitable one available. If another ETF with similar characteristics can be purchased that has a higher ranking in these two categories, it might be preferable to purchase that ETF. In any event, when trading options on ETFs with very low volume, the investor should always place limit orders rather than market orders on such options when trading. (See Chapter 9 on brokerage accounts for more information).

It is the intent of this book to focus on the use of covered call options with ETFs and not to lecture the reader/investor on the selection of specific ETFs or the need for diversification in one's portfolio. It is assumed that the reader/investor understands and has employed the concept of balancing a portfolio between equity investments, fixed income investments, cash and other alternative investments. Also, despite the diversification inherent in ownership of an

ETF, it is also assumed that the investor will balance the equity portion of the portfolio with at least several different ETFs to give the total equity portfolio a broad cross diversification between industry sectors and indexes as well as perhaps participations in international markets and differing investment styles. Researching the information available on www.amex.com or www.nasdaq.com and ordering prospectuses should give the investor the background needed to make quality investment decisions about individual ETFs.

COVERED CALL OPTION
WRITING ON ETFs

To really understand what *you* will be doing through covered call option writing we need to start by looking first at a typical call transaction from the *buyer's* perspective. That side of the transaction has absolutely nothing directly to do with what you will be doing, but understanding the "buy" side of the transaction will greatly help you understand the "sell" side, which is *your* side. For purposes of simplicity, commissions will not be included in any of the following examples. Later we will discuss how you can keep commissions down to a reasonable minimum. But for now, just remember that there will be some commissions involved that will affect these numbers a bit.

THE CALL BUYER'S (SPECULATOR'S)
SIDE OF THE TRANSACTION

Let's say a hypothetical ETF we will call KKK Biotech Fund ("**ticker symbol**" "KKK") is selling for $50 per share at the end of January. "John," as we will call the buyer, thinks KKK may be poised to rise, so he buys ten KKK call contracts with a June expiration and with a strike price of $55 per share. For this he pays a premium of, let's say, $3 per contract. Each call contract covers 100 shares of the underlying ETF, unless later adjusted for a stock split or stock dividend. So during the term of this option John controls 1,000 shares of KKK. The price he pays for this, the option premium, is $3,000 ($3 premium per contract x 10 contracts x 100 shares per contract).

The price of the option is based on mathematical formulations and largely revolves around the price volatility of the underlying ETF, how far the strike price of the option is from the current price of the ETF, and how much time exists between now and the time the option will expire.

The more volatile a given ETF's recent price history in the marketplace, the higher the premium a call will command. For example, all other things being equal, a call on many of the high-flying tech ETFs, which experience substantial price swings, would typically have a premium greater than KKK Biotech Fund's options. In turn, KKK Biotech Fund's options would logically have a premium that would be higher than a less volatile ETF...say, for example, a public utility ETF.

Second, the price of the ETF relative to the strike price of the option is a major factor. If the price of KKK is $50 per share, it only needs to trade $5 per share higher to reach a $55 strike price, while it would need to trade $10 higher to reach a $60 strike price. Since the likelihood is obviously much greater of the ETF price reaching $55 by the end of the same expiration period than $60, the price of the option for a $55 strike will be significantly higher than the $60 strike. In other words, for out-of-the-money calls, the closer the strike price is to the current market price of the ETF, the greater the call option premium will be.

Third, if it is now March and you are writing an option, you will want a larger premium for a call that will expire in September than one that will expire in June. If you are giving the call buyer the option to buy your ETF at a specific price until September, the buyer has a lot more time for the price to go up than if the option expires in June. For that reason, the buyer will have to pay quite a bit more for the September expiration than for the June expiration

The mathematical formulas are the framework behind the pricing of options for both buyer and seller. Ultimately, actual trading prices are established by what a willing buyer and willing seller agree upon.

Another factor that can affect the level of option premiums is the economic environment. For example, let's say there is a rough market where prices have declined, recovered a bit, declined, and so on. There isn't much "visibility" going forward regarding when the economy will improve and equity prices will recover. That scenario is reflected not only in ETF prices, but also in option premiums. Option premiums for the same ETFs, strike prices and expirations, when compared with different economic times, have sometimes trended lower during these times of market uncertainty. In other words, the premiums you receive from writing options in that economic climate may not be quite as large as they were when the economy was more certain and the markets were performing better. The good news is that an investor can still find very acceptable option premiums to reach target investment objectives, and it is possible that when the economy improves and markets recover option premiums will improve as well, providing even better returns from option writing.

Getting back to the KKK example, how does this work for John? The buyer of a call is a speculator. In this case John is speculating that the price of KKK will rise fairly quickly so he can take his profit. The call he has purchased will go up and down with the price of KKK.

These option contracts, just like the underlying ETF, both continue to be traded on the open market. In the short run, if the price of KKK would rise, then the price of the call contract should rise as well. And the price of the option would rise at a higher percentage rate than the ETF itself, because the purchase of an option provides "**leverage**"...100 shares for each contract. In this case, for a price of $3,000 John has control, for a limited period of time, of 1,000 shares of KKK worth $50,000. If KKK would rise to $55 the next day after the trade, the owner of the ETF would have a gain for that day of 10%. The call option, however, might in turn rise to $4.50 or a gain of 50% above the option purchase price. The buyer, if he wished to, could then sell his option contracts on the open market and pocket his gain on the transaction. This really has no effect on you and your option strategy. You will almost always just sit on your covered call options and wait for the expiration date to pass.

And, if John wants to sell his calls, this doesn't affect you at all. Specific buyers and sellers of calls aren't matched together unless calls are assigned at expiration. Either party can get out of their call position through their broker, just like an ETF trade. That's what makes options fungible.

This demonstrates the reason why a speculator might choose to buy an option rather than buy the underlying ETF. Had John purchased 1,000 shares of KKK at $50 and sold it at $55 his investment would have been $50,000 and his profit $5,000 for a return of 10%. By buying the option contracts instead, he realized a 50% profit on his investment but tied up only $3,000 of his capital in the process. This sounds terrific, but what's the downside? If KKK had declined from $50 to $45 the value of his options would also decline, perhaps going from $3 to $1.50. This would represent a loss of $1,500 or 50% of his investment. Had he bought the ETF and it declined to $45, the percentage loss would only be 10%.

By comparing ownership of ETF shares with ownership of ETF options one can begin to see the highly speculative nature of *buying* calls. Using options, a person can control a very large number of shares with very little money when compared with ownership of the underlying ETF itself. This means the potential for big gains and big losses. There's another major difference between buying an option versus buying the ETF. Options expire, but ETFs do not. If an option buyer continues to hold the option, and if the price of the ETF doesn't exceed the option "strike price" at expiration, the options will always be completely worthless. So, if an investor is a buyer of call options, he not only has to be right about the ETF going up, he has to be right about *when* it goes up!

This is a good time to introduce two more terms..."intrinsic value" and "time value" of options. The terms "in-the-money," "out-of-the-money" and "at-the-money" were discussed previously, which have to do with the relationship between the option strike price and the current market value of the ETF on which options are being written. The "intrinsic value" portion of an option's price is the dollar amount by which the strike price is less than the market price of the ETF. For example, if an ETF is trading at $47 ½ per share and the strike price of an option is $45, then the intrinsic value of the option is $2 ½. If the ETF price and the strike price are the same, then the intrinsic value is $0. It is also $0 if the strike price is any amount greater than the market price. Obviously this can change at any given moment as the price of an ETF moves up or down in trading. The strike price of a specific option is fixed until its expiration, but the market prices of the ETF and the option normally change constantly as trading takes place. So a given option premium can have intrinsic value at times when the market price of the ETF goes above the strike price and have no intrinsic value at times as well. You will generally write options where the strike price is greater than the market price of the ETF at the time of the trade, so there will be no intrinsic value when the option contracts are written.

The "time value" of an option premium is the market price of the option less the amount of intrinsic value. In other words, it is the value of the time remaining until the option expires. The longer the time between the current date and the expiration date the greater the time value of the option. This can be best understood through examples.

Assume the following facts. You have written a call option on an ETF we will call AAA. The strike price is $55, the current market value of the ETF is $57 and the current price of the option is $4 ¼. Since the market value is higher than the strike price, the intrinsic value is determined by subtracting the strike price from the market price, which gives an intrinsic value of $2 for the premium. The time value is then determined by taking the current option price of $4 ¼ and subtracting the intrinsic value. The time value is therefore $4 ¼ minus $2 or $2 ¼. Another way to say this is that the *intrinsic value is the amount by which the ETF is in-the-money*. The *time value is the rest of the price of the option*.

Let's look at a second example. You have written a call option on an ETF we will call JJJ. The strike price is $80, the current market value of the ETF is $76 and the current price of the option is $3. The option is out-of-the-money, so there is no intrinsic value. Thus, the entire market price of the option premium of $3 is regarded as time value. Obviously this changes as the price of the ETF and the option go up and down.

Back to KKK Biotech Fund again. John stands to realize a substantial percentage profit or loss on his call option investment if there are short-term swings up or down in the market value of KKK. Let's examine what will happen if John continues to hold his option until the expiration date in June. You will recall that the strike price of the option contract John bought was $55. This means that on the expiration date if the price of KKK is less than $55 the options expire with no value. John has lost his entire investment. Why? John's option contracts give him the right, but not the obligation, to buy 1,000 shares of KKK for $55 per share at any time through the June expiration date. Options always expire on the Saturday following the third Friday of the expiration month. Generally options are not exercised until the expiration date and then, of course, only if they are in-the-money. The reason for that is simple. Option buyers are often speculators who really don't want to own the ETF on a long-term basis or at all. Therefore, if the buyer of the option wants to close out his option position before the expiration, the buyer will almost always sell the contracts on the open market rather than exercise the options and then wait to sell the ETF after it is delivered to his broker.

But, in this case we are assuming John has not sold his option contracts and the June expiration date has just passed. We have said that if the price of KKK is below $55 he has lost his entire investment. What happens if after the expiration date the ETF is above $55 per share? As we just said, John would have typically sold his contracts before expiration, but if the expiration date passes and the underlying ETF market price is greater than the strike price, John should exercise his options and buy the ETF because the options have intrinsic value. Let's say the price of KKK is $57 at the close of the market on the expiration date. If John exercises his options he will pay $55,000 for his 1,000 shares of KKK. By exercising his options he will have $57,000 worth of KKK which he can sell for a $2,000 profit.

But didn't John pay $3,000 for the options and won't he still have a net loss by exercising the options and selling the ETF? Yes...but the gain on the sale of the ETF will partially offset the loss of the premium he paid ($2,000 investment gain - $3,000 premium loss = $1,000 net loss).

Again, if John had held his options until around the expiration date he would have most likely sold the contracts themselves rather than exercise the options and sell the ETF. Why? It is a much simpler transaction. By the time he could take delivery of the ETF and sell it, the market price could possibly go down. If the ETF was trading at $57 towards the end of the day on the last day of trading before expiration, the $55 KKK call option would be trading at about $2 per contract (time is up, so there is only the $2 intrinsic value and no time value is left). He would receive about $2,000 when he sold his ten contracts ($2 x 10 x 100), for the same result (except for commissions).

When you remember that about eighty-percent of all options contracts that are out-of-the-money when the transaction is initiated expire worthless, it becomes clear that buying options is highly speculative. It requires significant price movement occurring rather quickly in the underlying ETF if the buyer is to make a profit, especially if there isn't much time remaining to expiration.

It is also clear that in many cases much or all of the option buyer's investment can be lost, even if the price of the underlying ETF rises somewhat before the expiration date.

Let's use the example of John's KKK options again. We'll say the price of KKK Biotech Fund goes from $50 to $54 ¾ at expiration and John still holds his options. Even though the price of KKK has increased by $4 ¾, or 9.5%, in just about five months, John has still lost his entire investment. He would not exercise his option to buy shares at $55 that can be bought on the open market for $54 ¾. He has lost the premium he paid for the options. What is John's breakeven point on the expiration date? If he paid $3 per share premium to buy each contract, and if the strike price is $55, then John's breakeven is $58 per share ($3 + $55 = $58). In other words, if John holds the options through the expiration date, unless the price of KKK is at least $58 per share, or 16% higher than when he bought the options, he lost money. Of course, he could have sold the contracts well before the expiration date and made or lost money, depending on what the price of KKK and his options were and also how much of his time had run out before expiration.

It should be apparent why the opposite, mirror side of this transaction, fortunately the side in which you will be involved as a covered call writer, is the more attractive proposition.

THE CALL WRITER'S (YOUR) SIDE OF THE TRANSACTION

Let's look at the same transaction from YOUR side now. You are the owner of 1,000 shares of KKK Biotech Fund. You would like to increase your income by writing some call options on the shares you own. While you like the fund's long-term prospects, you doubt that the price of the ETF will go any higher than $5 above its current market price of about $50 over the next few months. It is about the end of January and you start checking out the premiums for KKK options contracts with various different strike prices and expiration dates. One of them that looks attractive to you is the June $55 KKK call. It is trading at, again, let's say, $3 per contract. For receiving a premium of $3 per share you decide you would be willing to let go of your 1,000 shares of KKK at $55 per share if the price should be greater than $55 on the expiration date. Remember that the option buyer could call your shares away from you at any time up to and including the expiration date, but this rarely ever happens before the expiration date, even if the market price of the ETF goes above the strike price.

Using your computer, you plug all the data into the Excel option spreadsheet mentioned earlier and read the information as follows:

DATE------>		29-Jan					
X	X	X		X	X	X	
CO.	#	SHARE	MARKET		OPTION		
SYM.	SHS.	PRICE	VALUE	DIV.	EXPIR.	STRIKE	DAYS
KKK	1,000	$50.00	$50,000	$0.64	15-Jun	$55.00	137

X	X	X						
			$	PREM.		TOTAL	MAX.	ANNUAL
CO.	OPTION		PREM.	$ PER	CONT.	ANNUAL	CAP.	YIELD W/
SYM.	SYMBOL	PREM.	INC.	DAY	YIELD	YIELD	APP.	CAP. APP.
KKK	KKKFJ	$3.00	$3,000	$21.90	6.00%	17.27%	$5,000	43.91%

From this transaction you will collect $3,000 in option writing income ($3 premium per share x 10 contracts x 100 shares per contract, not including commissions). You see that, on an annualized basis, the premium income and dividends at the current market price of KKK will yield 17.27%. Not bad! And it will be locked in until June 15 (the third Friday in June) based upon that premium and the market price of the ETF on the day of the transaction. The significance of the annualized yield will be discussed again later. It is used for comparison purposes, as investors are used to thinking in annual terms. When you buy a six-month CD at the bank at a 5% rate of interest, for example, the rate quoted is on an annual basis. If they quoted you 2 ½% for the six months, that would be comparable to the contract yield of 6% in this example.

You also have the potential to realize an additional $5,000 of capital appreciation if the ETF goes up to or over $55 per share on the expiration date. You can see that the total return on an annualized basis, which is the premium income, plus dividends, plus additional capital appreciation if the ETF is called away from you at expiration, is 43.91%.

Now the downside. If KKK Biotech Fund would go to, say, $60 before the expiration date, you would probably feel pretty bad that you had lost out on some additional capital appreciation. You would only receive $55 per share plus your option premium of $3, or a total of $58 per share, so you would have missed out on receiving $2 per share that your ETF would have been worth had you done nothing but hold it. Yet you realized an annualized return well into double digits. You also had $3 per share of downside protection if KKK's price had headed south. Some transactions will turn out like that. Just remember that as a covered call writer you are no longer in the business of maximizing capital appreciation on any given ETF. You are in the business of using covered call options to provide you a rate of return that will meet or exceed your objective. If you keep that in mind, you will not be disappointed, even if your ETF is called away from you at times. An even more frequent occurrence would be that your ETF is called away, but the strike price plus the premium you receive is greater than the market value of the ETF at expiration. This means you are better off than if you had just held the ETF.

This points out that we can't just look at the call option premium income in isolation. We have to consider what happens to the ETF price too in figuring the overall return. Obviously it can go down too, which will be addressed shortly.

So, you decide to go ahead and place an order to "sell-to-open" ten contracts of the KKK June $55 calls at $3. You are not buying the calls, you are selling to someone the right to buy your shares at a specific price and over a specific time period. And this is the opening of the transaction for you, so it is referred to as "sell-to-open," or your broker may call it "sell covered call." If you decided later that you wanted to close out the transaction rather than wait for the options to expire or be exercised on the expiration date, you would then do the opposite and enter an order to "buy-to-close." That would close out the transaction. This is hardly ever recommended, and will be discussed in more detail at an appropriate point.

When you have entered your order, John or some other buyer buys your contracts through his broker and pays

$3,000. The deal is settled and you get the money placed into your brokerage account *the next day*. The reason you receive the premium income now is that the buyer obviously has to pay for the buy side of the transaction immediately, and you are the lucky beneficiary of immediate cash when you are on the sell side of the transaction. You are free to immediately withdraw that money, let it sit, or invest it in something else that will also produce more income and capital gain opportunity.

So what do you do after you have sold your calls? Almost always, you will just sit on them and wait for the expiration date to occur. Some other alternatives will be discussed later, but mostly you will just wait it out until expiration. You can look forward to each passing day, as time is the best friend of an option writer. Every day that ticks off toward the expiration date means you are closer to the time you can either write a new option on your ETF or you will receive cash for your ETF at the strike price.

Let's assume for a moment that the market price of KKK Biotech Fund remains at $50 on the expiration date. What happens? Since a buyer would not pay the higher strike price for an ETF that he could buy at a lower price on the open market, the options expire unexercised. You have previously pocketed the buyer's $3,000 and you get to keep your ETF. Now you can write more call options. With the ETF price the same, if you write another one to expire in about the same time period later, you will likely receive a similar amount of option writing income as the previous transaction. In fact, if you were to do that for an entire year and the price of KKK shares would remain at $50 at the end of the year, you would have received a return of over 17% from your premium income...a nice gain in a flat market. An owner of KKK Biotech Fund shares who did not write options would have no gain at all. Hopefully you are able to see what is meant about option writing working its magic in a flat to slowly rising market.

And if KKK shares closed above $55 on the June expiration date you would receive $55,000 and could then use the proceeds as you please. A serious option writer would probably buy more ETF shares and then write more option contracts. The cycle goes on and on.

If your KKK ETF closed between $50 and $55...say $54...you still get to keep all of your option premium *and* your KKK shares, as the price of the ETF was still not above the $55 strike price on the expiration date. The nice thing about this is that you have kept your ETF, but it is now worth more than when you wrote your option in January ($54 vs. $50). Not only do you have a gain in the ETF, but when you write your next option contracts, say the September contract, you will find that the $55 strike price contracts will be trading at a higher relative price, adjusted for the difference in time to expiration...perhaps $4. This is because the market price is closer to the strike price now than it was the last time you wrote the option contracts. Remember that for out-of-the-money calls, the closer the market price is to the strike price, the higher the option premium will be. This time your ten contracts would give you about $4,000 of premium income...and for even less time to expiration.

Another strategy that might be effectively used in this case would be to write contracts at a higher strike price...for example the $60 contract instead of the $55 contract. This would reduce your premium income because the strike price is higher, but it would allow for more room for the price to increase in KKK by the next selected expiration date. The strike price you select will largely be based on what you think may happen to the ETF price by the next selected expiration date. Of course, that is very difficult to know, but the investor usually has some informed thoughts on the subject from what you hear and read.

But what occurs if the price of KKK went down. That's when "bad" is really "not quite so bad." Let's say at the June expiration KKK shares are trading at $48. You have the premium income of $3,000 to keep and obviously you get to keep your ETF, because the buyer of the call would not pay you $55 per share for ETF that could be bought on the open market for $48. Since you received $3 per share in premium income, you have a $1 net gain per share in the transaction from the date the contracts were written ($48 + $3 - $50). You have fared far better than a shareholder that simply owned the ETF and did not write options on it. You have had $3 per share of downside protection, which is somewhat like insurance, during the entire term of the contract until expiration. Of course, if KKK went down even further than that, you could experience an overall loss, but a loss that would be less than if you hadn't written the option contracts.

What would you do then after the expiration of the options with your $48 KKK shares? There are several things you could do, depending on how you feel about the ETF's prospects and what is going on in the market and the economy in general. These are your choices:

If you believe your ETF has significant near-term recovery potential:

- Simply hold the ETF and do not write options for awhile, allowing the ETF to rise without it being called away.

or

- Write calls that are further out-of-the-money...that is, write calls with a strike price that is significantly higher than the current market price. You won't get a huge premium, but you will get some. And the likelihood of your shares being called away is greatly reduced if the price of the ETF goes up.

If you believe your ETF has significant further near-term loss potential:

- Sell your ETF now and wait for a better investment climate for this ETF or another one.

or

- Write calls that have a strike price that is only slightly above or perhaps even somewhat below the current market price...the in-the-money option contracts. This will provide you with much better premium income and therefore a lot more downside protection. Again, it is almost never recommended that you write in-the-money calls, where the strike price is below the market price. If you are wrong and the price of the ETF goes up, you will have your ETF called away at a price that may not be acceptable to you. So, this is the only time that you should ever consider such a strategy...and be sure you really believe that your ETF has a strong chance of declining in value below the strike price of your options.

If you believe your ETF's price will meander about where it is or go up a bit:

- Treat this as a normal option writing opportunity, because this is when option writing works its best magic. You may wish to write call contracts with a shorter-term expiration and also try to ratchet the strike prices up at expirations if the ETF is gradually increasing in value so you get back to the position you were in originally.

Remember...it is still possible to lose money buying ETFs and writing call options if the price of your ETF declines significantly. But if you are caught in a declining market where your shares are going down in price, you will *always* be better off if you have written calls on your shares compared with just owning the stock alone, because the premium income gives you the added downside price protection "insurance."

A CALL OPTION WRITER'S DREAM

What would be the optimum situation for an option writer to maximize gain opportunities? This is difficult to achieve, but as an option writer you will have this happen to you on occasion to some degree or another with some of your ETF shares. The optimum situation is to write calls so that on the expiration date the market value of the shares is just under the strike price. In addition to the premium income you keep your ETF, so you can write new options at a higher strike price and continue to do this over and over again at each expiration date if the ETF price keeps slowly rising. In this perfect world you would receive steady premium income, but by keeping your ETF as it goes up to a price just below your strike price, your shares become increasingly worth more too.

Let's review a highly embellished example. You buy JJJ shares at $50 and write contracts on them at a strike price of $55 and receive a premium of $3. On expiration your ETF is trading at $54 ¾, so you write more options at a $60 strike price and receive $2 ½ in premium income. At the next expiration the ETF is trading at $59 ½. You write more options at a $65 strike price, and this time you get $2 ¼ in premium income per share. One more time. At this expiration your ETF is trading at $64, so you write the $70 strike price and get $2 in option premium income. At the expiration your ETF is trading right at $70. How did you do? Well, you paid $50 for shares that are now worth $70. In addition, you have collected $9 ¾ in premium income. You total gain from start to finish is $29 ¾ per share. You are way ahead of your colleagues who have only bought the

ETF and held onto it with a $20 per share gain. Of course, they have never had to worry about having their ETF called away from them. But don't forget, you've had quite a bit of downside price protection too in case the shares started heading south, and a lot more predictability in your overall return as you collected all of those option premiums.

Should you be concerned when the prices of your ETFs move above the strike price or when your shares get called away from you at expiration? Don't worry about having your shares called away from you. As an investor who owns solid ETFs, your goal is to achieve an above average return on a consistent basis by writing call option contract premiums on your ETF shares. That's your game...that's the business you are in as an investor. You should be very happy if all the shares you write options on were called away from you at every option expiration date. That way you wouldn't have any losses and you would be achieving your most optimistic objective, premium income and capital appreciation too, every time. Between your premium income, dividends and capital appreciation, you would be doing extremely well...returns well into double digits and likely well beyond what Warren Buffett has achieved over the long haul.

Is there a risk that you end up having all of your best performing ETFs called away from you with only the losers remaining in your portfolio? That doesn't seem to be the experience. Whether you are writing call options or just buying ETFs to hold, you should never buy an ETF that you aren't comfortable holding for the long term. And you should never buy an ETF just because it would give you a lot of premium income. That implies it's a volatile ETF, meaning that it has more downside potential in a bad market as it does upside potential in a good market.

You also have to keep in mind that when you write call options you are dealing with a rather short time horizon for the option. In most cases you won't be writing three-year LEAPS on your ETFs that would provide a lot of time for the ETF to go up significantly. You could write a long-term option in an isolated case for diversification, but that would probably be the exception rather than the rule. For shorter-term options, there usually just isn't enough time for an ETF to go way beyond the strike price, particularly if you leave some room for capital appreciation by writing out-of-the-money calls. That's not to say that it can't happen. It will, on occasion. Of course, when the ETF is called away from you, you can simply buy it back again and either hold it or write more calls on it. It will cost you more to buy it back the second time than it did the first time, but you will have the premium income to help too. On occasion you will find the opposite happen, where you have your ETF called away from you and then the price goes down so that you can buy it back for less than the strike price at which it was earlier called away. Obviously there are a lot of different ways this can go.

The most important thing is that you buy ETFs that make you comfortable and you stick with them until there is a reason to sell them. And if one of your ETFs is called away, you should always ask yourself if you should buy the same ETF back again, or if there is another ETF on your working list that meets your criteria for investment.

The possibility of missing out on a good sized gain isn't too much of a price to pay when you consider all of the advantages that writing covered calls offers.

The hypothetical scenarios discussed here will not happen to you in the way they were described. They have simply been included for purposes of understanding what an optimum objective might be. But with common sense in your ETF picking and the tools this program offers, you will soon find yourself well on your way to selecting option writing opportunities that will provide you with solid double-digit returns. Good cocktail party conversation material in these difficult times!

SELECTING CALL WRITING
OPTION ALTERNATIVES

At the back of this book is a diskette for PC use. One of the templates it contains is a Microsoft® Excel spreadsheet file named "calls." You will find it a significant and useful resource to assist in making decisions on which call options to write for the ETFs you own. It provides a wealth of information to simplify decision-making and saves a lot of time in "crunching the numbers," although the same analysis can also be done manually with the worksheets supplied in the Appendix of this book.

On the next page you will find examples of different option writing choices on six different hypothetical ETFs. For each ETF the same strike price has been chosen that would allow for some capital appreciation (out-of-the-money calls), also using three different expiration dates for each ETF. These examples will clearly point out how returns vary depending on the expiration dates selected.

Let's discuss these worksheets in detail, because you will use this same format over and over again in making your option writing decisions.

Note the row towards the top with the small "x"s. In any vertical column where there is an "x," that means you need to supply the information yourself. If there isn't an "x" in a column, the information in that column is automatically calculated for you.

SAME STRIKE PRICE,
DIFFERENT EXPIRATION DATES

DATE---------->	6-Jul					
X	X	X	X	X	X	
CO.	#	SHARE	MARKET		OPTION	
SYM.	SHS.	PRICE	VALUE	D IV.	EXPIR.	STRIKE	DAYS
BBB	3,000	$16.79	$50,370	$0.00	17-Aug	$20.00	42
BBB	3,000	$16.79	$50,370	$0.00	19-Oct	$20.00	105
BBB	3,000	$16.79	$50,370	$0.00	18-Jan	$20.00	196
JJJ	1,200	$43.40	$52,080	$0.88	17-Aug	$45.00	42
JJJ	1,200	$43.40	$52,080	$0.88	19-Oct	$45.00	105
JJJ	1,200	$43.40	$52,080	$0.88	18-Jan	$45.00	196
KKK	1,100	$46.89	$51,579	$0.64	17-Aug	$50.00	42
KKK	1,100	$46.89	$51,579	$0.64	21-Sep	$50.00	77
KKK	1,100	$46.89	$51,579	$0.64	21-Dec	$50.00	168
TTT	1,000	$50.41	$50,410	$0.72	17-Aug	$52.50	42
TTT	1,000	$50.41	$50,410	$0.72	19-Oct	$52.50	105
TTT	1,000	$50.41	$50,410	$0.72	18-Jan	$52.50	196

X	X	X						
			$	PREM.		TOTAL	MAX.	ANNUAL
CO.	OPTION		PREM.	$ PER	CONT.	ANNUAL	CAP.	YIELD W/
SYM.	SYMBOL	PREM.	INC.	DAY	YIELD	YIELD	APP.	CAP. APP.
BBB	BBBHD	$0.55	$1,650	$39.29	3.28%	28.47%	$9,630	194.62%
BBB	BBBJD	$1.30	$3,900	$37.14	7.74%	26.92%	$9,630	93.37%
BBB	BBBAD	$2.10	$6,300	$32.14	12.51%	23.29%	$9,630	58.90%
JJJ	JJJHI	$0.70	$840	$20.00	1.61%	16.04%	$1,920	48.08%
JJJ	JJJJI	$1.60	$1,920	$18.29	3.69%	14.84%	$1,920	27.66%
JJJ	JJJAI	$2.55	$3,060	$15.61	5.88%	12.97%	$1,920	19.83%
KKK	KKKHJ	$1.00	$1,100	$26.19	2.13%	19.90%	$3,421	77.54%
KKK	KKKIJ	$1.65	$1,815	$23.57	3.52%	18.05%	$3,421	49.49%
KKK	KKKLJ	$2.95	$3,245	$19.32	6.29%	15.03%	$3,421	29.44%
TTT	TTTHX	$1.20	$1,200	$28.57	2.38%	22.12%	$2,090	58.15%
TTT	TTTJX	$2.00	$2,000	$19.05	3.97%	15.22%	$2,090	29.63%
TTT	TTTAX	$3.25	$3,250	$16.58	6.45%	13.43%	$2,090	21.16%

Many of the columns are obvious. The first column is the ETF ticker symbol on the exchange where the ETF is listed...the American Exchange or the NASDAQ. There are three rows for each symbol because three different call writing calculations have been included for each ETF. The next column is the number of shares you own and then the current market price of the ETF. What was done here was to put down the number of shares that would approximate an investment ownership of about $50,000 in each ETF for consistency. It was rounded to the nearest hundred shares, as an option contract always applies to one hundred shares of ETF, also called a **"round lot."** So each option contract covers one hundred shares. You can't write options for an **"odd lot,"** which is less than one hundred shares.

The dollar amount invested in an ETF for covered call writing is not particularly material. The absolute most important thing is that you purchase in round lots, regardless of the amount you are investing. The more round lots you purchase, the more cost efficiency there is in brokerage commissions on option trades, which will be discussed in detail in another chapter.

CALCULATING COVERED CALL WRITING OPPORTUNITIES

The market value column doesn't have an "x," so that means the calculation there is automatic if you have entered the other information. Next you would enter the annual dividend payment per share of ETF. A lot of ETFs these days don't pay any or only a small dividend, but whatever it is if you enter the annual dividends per share it will calculate them in with the other information to figure your total investment yields.

The column on option expiration deserves more detailed discussion. We've briefly said that there several dozen ETFs at this time on which you are able to write covered call options. For any given ETF, there is typically a variety of option expiration dates to choose from. Let's just take the DIAMONDS Trust Series 1 (symbol: DIA) as an example. In early October there were options available expiring in October, November, December, January, March, June, September and the LEAPS the following January, and a year from that January...several months over two years away. This gives investors quite a few choices to suit their own unique call option writing needs. More detail will be provided on how those selections are made, but at this point suffice it to know that you would often have quite a selection to choose from in making your option writing decisions. For any given ETF, there is an "option cycle" which means that generally there are options expiring on the same four months every year plus the current and the next following month. Some offer LEAPS as well. Not all ETFs, however, offer this many months in their option cycle.

There are three different cycles, and they are set as follows:

Cycle 1:	January	April	July	October
Cycle 2:	February	May	August	November
Cycle 3:	March	June	September	December

In the chapter on brokerage accounts, details will be provided about how to determine what option expiration dates are available to you and how you get quotes on them and other information to plug into the worksheet.

One thing that is always true, however, is that all ETFs on which options can be traded offer an expiration for the current month and the next month. So, the October options would not be available for KKK if it were only February. But when we are in the month of September, there will be a September and an October option for KKK…simply because there is always an option created with an expiration for the current and the following month.

The next column also deserves some extensive discussion…the strike price. The strike price is the part of the option contract that specifies the price at which the option buyer has the right to buy your ETF up through the expiration date. When the market price of any given ETF goes up and down, the exchange where the option contracts are traded will open up new strike prices if they have not already been opened previously. So if shares of JJJ have traded recently from a low of $30 per share to a high of $80, there would be strike prices offered at least in $5 increments from $30 through $80.

As you know by now, what is typically recommended is to select a strike price above the price where the ETF is currently trading…the out-of-the-money calls. That will hopefully insure receipt of an option premium that will fulfill your yield objective and also provide the opportunity for at least some capital appreciation if the ETF goes up in value. You should usually select at least two different strike prices above the current market value of the ETF and put those numbers onto the worksheet with the other information to help determine which is the one that works best for you considering the rate of return, the capital appreciation potential and the time to expiration.

The column titled "Days," which shows the number of days from the current date through the date of expiration, is automatically calculated. When you enter the option expiration date, the number of days from the current date is subtracted from the expiration date with the resulting number of days placed into this column. So, for example, for the BBB option expiring October 19 there are 105 days remaining from the date the worksheet was prepared through the expiration date, and so on.

The option symbol is the next column. You get that information from the broker you are using. It can easily be retrieved online or by a phone call.

(It is possible to determine the option symbol for many options other than going through a broker. Please see "How to Determine the Symbol for an Option" in the Appendix.)

Finally, you plug in the current quote for the option, which you will get from the broker as well. Sometimes there can be quite a bit of spread, or variance, between the "bid" and "ask" prices that are quoted for options. The bid price is what a buyer is currently bidding or willing to pay to buy the contract. The ask price is what a seller is currently asking or willing to sell the contract for. Actual trading will usually take place between those two figures. Generally it is best to take the bid and ask prices, add them together and divide by two to get the approximate midpoint. So, if the bid is $1.10 and the ask is $1.50, use the midpoint of $1.30, or perhaps even a little less for conservatism, and plug that figure into the worksheet under the "Prem." column. This is the premium per share that you could reasonably expect to receive if you placed an order, so it should be valid for your calculation purposes.

You will see the total premium income you would collect under the next column marked "$ Prem. Inc." The commissions obviously vary from broker to broker, so you can customize your own template to accommodate the charges for your brokerage accounts.

The next column, "Prem. $ Per Day" is simply the premium income you would receive on a given transaction divided by the number of days from the current date to the expiration date. This information might not be important to all option writing investors, but it is useful to compare it with other option writing opportunities.

Next is "Contract Yield," which gives you the immediate percentage return from the premium for this transaction only, and it is not annualized. In other words, it just tells you what percent return on your investment you would be getting right now. Again, another comparison technique.

The next column, "Total Annual Yield," combines the dividend income and also the premium income for the transaction and calculates the *yield on an annualized basis.* It's annualized because investors are used to thinking about our returns that way. For example, if you are seeking a 12% annual return you don't say you want a one-percent return per month, because people just don't think that way. So take the example of the BBB options expiring on October 19. What this means is that if you could continue to write the same option at the same premium price and with the same frequency...days to expiration...you would realize an annualized yield on your investment, based on its current value, of 26.92%, not including commissions. This would mean that at the October expiration date you would need to do the exact same deal again and again to get that precise yield. Obviously it isn't going to happen that way, because the price of the ETF will change, and that means the price of the options in the future will change too. But it is the best information we have at a given point in time, so that's why it's used. Obviously we can't predict where prices will be in the future, so we use the measurements we have now. That gives us the ability to compare one option opportunity with another in an "apples to apples" manner.

The next to the last column is the maximum capital appreciation that can be made on the transaction...that would be if the ETF is called away. Let's use the example again of the BBB options expiring in October. A writer sells 30 contracts of BBB on the 3,000 shares owned (30 times 100 = 3,000 shares) at a strike price of $20 per share. Since the price of the ETF is $16.79, that leaves a possible additional appreciation of capital of $3.21 per share if the ETF is selling for over $20 at the expiration date and is called away. Take $3.21 times 3,000 and you get $9,630, which is the number shown in that column. So then, if the ETF is called away at expiration, the writer would have realized capital appreciation of $9,630 plus the premium income of $3,900...no dividend income, since BBB doesn't pay a dividend...for a total of $13,530. If you divide that figure by the market value of the BBB shares and then annualize the combined return, you get a whopping 93.37%!

If you would say that doing this every 105 days, in the case of this option writing example, is extremely unlikely, you would be absolutely correct. But, again, making this total return computation simply allows us to make comparisons with other option writing opportunities, and for that purpose it is of great value to us. All of the work done with the template is done at a particular slice in time.

There is an instruction page in the Appendix outlining exactly what data to enter into the template to assess option opportunities and how to customize the template to fit your own brokerage commission schedule. Worksheets are included at the end of the book for use by those who are not using a computer. Though more laborious, with a pencil, calculator and a little patience, you would have access to exactly the same information as those who use the Excel template.

The next worksheet displays three different strike prices for each ETF that has been selected. These different strike prices would allow for an increasing amount of capital appreciation before the ETF would be called away. Just one common expiration date is used for each ETF. This will demonstrate how returns vary depending on the strike prices selected.

These are real examples of options that were available and the market prices for them. They represent actual trades that an investor might consider when the time comes to start writing options.

The subject of diversification was touched upon briefly and the fact that some ETFs are riskier than others, which means their ETF prices are more volatile. That volatility is reflected in call option prices too and the yield that an investor can expect from writing call options. For example, of the six ETFs profiled on these worksheets, the greatest annualized yield on the first worksheet would be for the BBB August $20 calls. The premium you would receive for this transaction would give you an annualized return of 28.47%. An observer of this sheet might ask why an investor should buy these other ETFs when that kind of a return can be obtained writing BBB options. The answer is that BBB has significantly more upward and downward price movements than the other shares, and balance is needed by buying other ETFs for broader equity diversification.

SAME OPTION EXPIRATION DATE,
DIFFERENT STRIKE PRICES

DATE——>		6-Jul					
X	X	X		X	X	X	
CO.	#	SHARE	MARKET		OPTION		
SYM.	SHS.	PRICE	VALUE	DIV.	EXPIR.	STRIKE	DAYS
BBB	3,000	$16.79	$50,370	$0.00	18-Jan	$20.00	196
BBB	3,000	$16.79	$50,370	$0.00	18-Jan	$22.50	196
BBB	3,000	$16.79	$50,370	$0.00	18-Jan	$25.00	196
JJJ	1,200	$43.40	$52,080	$0.88	18-Jan	$45.00	196
JJJ	1,200	$43.40	$52,080	$0.88	18-Jan	$47.50	196
JJJ	1,200	$43.40	$52,080	$0.88	18-Jan	$50.00	196
KKK	1,100	$46.89	$51,579	$0.64	18-Jan	$50.00	196
KKK	1,100	$46.89	$51,579	$0.64	18-Jan	$53.38	196
KKK	1,100	$46.89	$51,579	$0.64	18-Jan	$56.63	196
TTT	1,000	$50.41	$50,410	$0.72	18-Jan	$52.50	196
TTT	1,000	$50.41	$50,410	$0.72	18-Jan	$55.00	196
TTT	1,000	$50.41	$50,410	$0.72	18-Jan	$57.50	196

X	X	X						
			$	PREM.		TOTAL	MAX.	ANNUAL
CO.	OPTION		PREM.	$ PER	CONT.	ANNUAL	CAP.	YIELD W/
SYM.	SYMBOL	PREM.	INC.	DAY	YIELD	YIELD	APP.	CAP. APP.
BBB	BBBAD	$2.10	$6,300	$32.14	12.51%	23.29%	$9,630	58.90%
BBB	BBBAX	$1.45	$4,350	$22.19	8.64%	16.08%	$17,130	79.41%
BBB	BBBAE	$0.95	$2,850	$14.54	5.66%	10.54%	$24,630	101.60%
JJJ	JJJAI	$2.60	$3,120	$15.92	5.99%	13.18%	$1,920	20.05%
JJJ	JJJAW	$1.65	$1,980	$10.10	3.80%	9.11%	$4,920	26.70%
JJJ	JJJAJ	$1.00	$1,200	$6.12	2.30%	6.32%	$7,920	34.64%
KKK	WKKAJ	$3.25	$3,575	$18.24	6.93%	14.27%	$3,421	26.62%
KKK	WKKAX	$1.90	$2,090	$10.66	4.05%	8.91%	$7,134	34.67%
KKK	WKKAY	$1.05	$1,155	$5.89	2.24%	5.53%	$10,709	44.20%
TTT	TTTAX	$3.25	$3,250	$16.58	6.45%	13.43%	$2,090	21.16%
TTT	TTTAK	$2.05	$2,050	$10.46	4.07%	9.00%	$4,590	25.96%
TTT	TTTAY	$1.30	$1,300	$6.63	2.58%	6.23%	$7,090	32.42%

THE OPTION WRITING STRATEGY

What your overall goal should be is to take all of the ETFs in your portfolio and select option writing opportunities on them which will average out to an overall return at least as great as your objective. You will exceed that return in some cases, but in others you won't...especially if you try to leave room for significant additional capital appreciation. So, don't lose sight of the forest because of the trees. It's your *overall return* in a diversified, well-balanced ETF portfolio that counts.

Let's look at the figures on the first worksheet and use these as a means of strategizing about approaches to call option writing. The selection of option expirations has been narrowed down to just three and for only one strike price per ETF, but you need to remember that there are of lot more choices than those.

DIFFERENT EXPIRATIONS

Remember that there is always a call option that expires in the month following the current month for every optionable ETF. Those are obviously the shortest-term options available, except for the current month, and sometimes they are the best choice, especially in a rising market. If you select options that will expire in about one month, there isn't a whole lot of time between now and the expiration. If you leave room for at least a several point rise between the current ETF price and the strike price of the call option, the chance is less that the price will rise above the strike price to where the options would be exercised and your ETF called away from you. If there is, say, $4 between the current ETF price and the strike price, the chance of the ETF going up that much is a lot less for an option expiring in one month than it would be for one expiring in three months, six months or a year.

There's a logical progression in the price of the call option premium as the length of the time to expiration increases. You can see in all of the examples on this sheet that as the days to expiration become greater, the amount of the premium per contract increases. This will always be the case. The reason is this. If you are comparing options with various expirations using the same strike price, it makes sense that if you were a buyer of a call option you would be willing to pay more for one expiring in October than you would for one expiring two months earlier in August. That's because with the October contract the buyer has two more months for the ETF to possibly go up so he can profitably sell his option contract or exercise it at expiration.

As the number of days increases to expiration, *the rate of increase* in the amount of the premium tends to slow down. This causes a lot of option writers to stick more to the shorter term writing opportunities. This generally makes sense, although an option writer should usually try to have diversification in the expiration dates written on different ETFs in the portfolio. Shorter-term call options won't give you as much downside protection, however, as longer-term calls. So, the proper selection is dependent on your beliefs about what the near-term future holds.

As you can see, the premium for the BBB Technologies August call contract is a bit less than half that of the October contract. Yet the premium per day, the annual yield, and the annual yield with capital appreciation are all larger for the August contract. That is simply a function of the shorter time period until expiration. The same is true in comparing the October contract with the following January contract.

Let's say you have just written an out-of-the-money covered call on an ETF. And let's further say that the price of the underlying ETF remains exactly the same during the entire period until the option expires (this obviously won't happen, but will help make an important point). One might expect that the price of the option would decline in a straight line progression over its life until it expires worthless on the expiration date...like this.

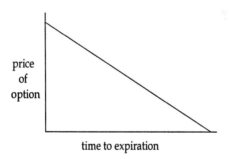

time to expiration

That's not typically the way things work, however. Usually the time value of an option retains more of its value until it gets closer to the expiration date. Thus, if the ETF price were to remain exactly the same, for a three month call option, for example, the decline in the price of the option as it gets closer and closer to the date of expiration might look something more like this.

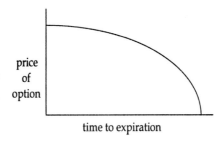

time to expiration

As you can see, with a flat ETF price the option holds more if its value until closer to expiration. An option writer could take some advantage of this by buying back calls to close just before expiration, say when the price of the option is only a small fraction of the original price when it was written. It wouldn't cost too much to buy them back at this time, and then the investor can write a new option at a higher premium with a longer time period to the next expiration than if the investor had simply waited for the first option to expire. The primary disadvantage of doing this is that the investor will pay additional commissions when the options are bought to close, which increases the overall cost. That's the reason why holding the options until expiration is almost always recommended. Some brokerages, however, reduce their commission costs quite a bit for option trades when the price on them is very low, which helps if you want to buy to close.

What are the advantages of writing shorter-term covered calls and the advantages of writing longer-term covered calls? Let's do an assessment:

Advantages of writing shorter-term covered calls

- Less likelihood of your ETF being called away from you at expiration because there is less time for the price to go up beyond the strike price.
- Greater yield on investment, given the time period of the transaction.
- Greater opportunity for more capital appreciation on the underlying ETF, as you may be able to increase the strike price in future option writing opportunities if the ETF price increases gradually.

Advantages of writing longer-term covered calls

- Larger total premium that will be available to you when credited to your account the next day.
- Less brokerage commissions, because you won't be writing new contracts as often if the expiration periods are longer. If you were writing only one month options, you would incur three times the brokerage commissions compared with writing options with three month expirations.
- More downside protection in the event of a decline in the price of the underlying ETF since the premium is greater on longer-term options.
- Less administrative work, since you only have to research option writing opportunities, handle trades and do record keeping as often as options expire.
- Ability to do some tax planning by selecting options that expire in the next tax year (more on this in another chapter).

Given the advantages of each, what should a call writing investor do? Here the subject of diversification again comes into play. Arguably the best strategy is to select a variety of expirations so that the options on your ETFs are not all expiring at once or in large amounts. That spreads out your yields to help you achieve your overall return objective, but it does something else very important.

There are some good reasons why you wouldn't want all of your options to expire on the same expiration date. If the equity markets were in a broad decline at the time of the expirations, you would be faced with a situation where your ETF prices were down a lot. You would have had some nice downside protection from the options that expired, but it could present some problems in writing your next set of options on your ETFs.

Let's demonstrate the problem with an exaggerated hypothetical example. Say you are diversified with five different ETFs. Let's also say that the difference between the price per share of these ETFs and the strike prices when you wrote your call options was a uniform $3 per share. That would have given you some pretty decent option writing income for the option period, regardless of when the expiration period is. The closer the market price of an ETF is to the strike price when you write a call option, the higher the premium will be. Now, let's say that all of your ETFs go down by $5 per share between the time you wrote your options and when the options expire. That means if you write a new set of options at the same strike prices you did before, the difference now between the market prices of your ETFs and the strike prices of your new options will be $8 per share. That's quite a bit greater than the $3 the last time you wrote options. This means that the option premiums and yields you will receive this time will be a whole lot less than the time before that. You would either have to accept much lower returns for that next option writing period, or you would have to reduce the strike prices when you write your next batch of contracts by $5 to give you a similar return. The problem with that is if the market starts to go up again significantly, your lower strike prices would mean that you would give up some of the upside appreciation in your ETFs. They might be called away from you on the next expiration date at a strike price $5 per share lower than the strike price you used in the first option expiration.

There's another reason you wouldn't want the same expiration on options for all of your ETFs. If there was a broad rally in the market, you might get a lot of your ETFs called away from you and be sitting with mostly cash at a time when the prices of ETFs are a lot higher. By diversifying into several different option expiration dates, it's a bit like buying a portfolio of diversified bonds with a variety of maturities, called a "bond ladder," so that you aren't faced with a large reinvestment situation at a time that may not be to your advantage.

Another diversification strategy would be to take shares in a single ETF and sell calls with different strike prices or expiration dates. For example, with 3,000 shares of BBB, you might write fifteen contracts with an October expiration and fifteen with a January expiration using the same strike price. Or, you might write fifteen contracts with a $20 strike price and fifteen contracts with a $22 ½ strike price using the same expiration date. It's just another way to broaden overall risk and reward exposure.

DIFFERENT STRIKE PRICES

What has been done with the second worksheet is to keep all of the option writing opportunities with the very same expiration date...namely, next January, which is over a half-year away. And the reason this has been done is to demonstrate the effect of selecting different strike prices. In these examples, the total annual yield won't be as exciting. As you will remember, the longer the time to expiration the lower the yield, even though the actual premium you receive is larger with a later expiration.

Let's take a look at the TTT examples. The ETF is trading at $50.41. The first strike selected is $52.50, which is the closest strike price available at this time above the current market price. The next higher one is $55 and then $57.50. We could select strike prices both higher and lower, but remember, we are trying to select opportunities that are both out-of-the-money and ones that will meet our overall double-digit return objective within our portfolio of ETFs.

Selecting from out-of-the-money options with the same expiration, the one that will always have the greatest premium and the highest total annual yield will be the one with a strike price closest to the market price...in this case the $52.50 strike price. You can see that at a premium of $3.25 it will provide a contract yield of 6.45%. Again, that's the actual yield of the option premium on this deal, but not annualized. Since we are looking at a little over a half-year to expiration, the contract yield is about half as large as the total annual yield of 13.43%.

The next component to look at is the capital appreciation that can be realized if the ETF goes up and what your overall yield will be if the ETF is called away from you at maturity. For the $52.50 strike price, the maximum capital appreciation that can be realized is $2,090...the strike price per share of $52.50 minus the current market price of $50.41 times the number of shares, which is all figured into the sheet. Your capital appreciation can't be any more if you write the $52.50 strike price, since the ETF will be called away from you at that price on expiration if the price is greater than that. If your ETF is called away, the annual yield with the capital appreciation is 21.16%...a very solid double-digit return.

As you look at a diversified portfolio of ETFs and call option expirations, if you decide to write some calls with expirations as far out as six months, this particular ETF and call option might suit your objective. It yields a double-digit return based on the market price of the ETF and the option today. It also gives you an opportunity for capital appreciation to get you to an annualized yield of over 21%. Of course, no one can know for sure what TTT will trade for a half-year from now. Over time equity investments tend to go up, so the odds may be fairly good that it will go up to $52.50 or above, in which case your 21+% projected return would be achieved. At least there's a greater chance of hitting the strike price with a half-year expiration than if you selected a one month call option. Obviously it could go to $52.50 within one month, or one day for that matter, but the odds of it going to $52.50 in a half-year are much greater than it going to that price in one month, as the long-term bias for equities is in an upward direction.

In fact, TTT might very well grow by more than that by the time a half-year is up. That's why in structuring an overall portfolio, an investor might look at a higher strike price, with the expectation that the value of the underlying ETF could grow more, and also accepting a lower call option premium. Let's look at the next opportunity. The next higher strike price is $55. At a premium of $2.05 it offers a 4.07% contract yield, and a 9% total annual yield, which is less than double-digit. But the capital appreciation opportunity goes from $2,090 with the $52.50 strike price to $4,590 with the $55 strike price. So, if your ETF were called away from you at $55 at the expiration, your annual yield including the capital appreciation would be 25.96%. To take this one step further, if you selected a strike price of $57.50, with a premium of $1.30 your contract yield would be 2.58% and the total annual yield would be 6.23%. But if your ETF were called away from you at $57.50 on expiration, your capital appreciation would go up to $7,090 and the annual yield including the capital appreciation would be 32.42%.

If you owned TTT and were looking today at writing call options on it, what would an investor's thinking process be in deciding what to do. The first thing is to be sure that such a long-term expiration fits into your overall plan for diversifying your call option portfolio. Another consideration would be what you think will happen to TTT's price in the next year. If you feel strongly that it has good appreciation potential, then you might opt for one of the higher strike prices to try to get the additional capital appreciation. As long as the total annual yield you select fits into the overall portfolio average to fit your return objective, then perhaps you go for the option offering greater capital appreciation.

If you really don't have a strong feeling about the ETF going up, then it might be best to just get the higher premium, because that will give you more cash income up front and a bit more insurance toward the downside too. A bird in the hand is worth two in the bush, as they say. Or, as Warren Buffett commented in his 2000 Berkshire Hathaway Annual Report, "A girl in a convertible is worth five in the phonebook!" [6]

Your decision must be balanced with the other things you are doing in your portfolio and with your outlook for each specific ETF. For example, with a higher yield on BBB calls you might settle for a lower yield, and more capital appreciation opportunity, on the TTT calls, but still reach an overall double-digit annualized yield. Some option writers always go with the closest out-of-the-money option to maximize the option writing income. Others like a higher strike price to get more of a balance between option writing income and capital appreciation opportunity. There's no single best way for everyone. Both are good, depending on what your objectives and needs are...and your outlook for the specific ETFs in your portfolio as well as economic conditions generally.

---

[6] "Chairman's Letter," Berkshire Hathaway 200 Annual Report: 14

As a general guideline, though, in assessing the relative attractiveness of option writing opportunities you should focus on the "Total Annual Yield" column the most. This is the annualized return based on current dividends and premiums. The capital appreciation may or may not materialize, so one should not get too starry eyed by the big percentages that appear in the last column.

It is important to remember that you are in the business of achieving your return objective by call option writing. If your ETFs were called away from you at every expiration, you might be missing some upside capital appreciation in certain cases, yet you would be meeting or exceeding your objective all the time, which is what you set out to do in the first place. That's the business you are in with your ETF investments and option writing program...and you should stick to it.

FOR HIGH RISK SEEKERS: USING VOLATILITY AND MARGIN

Some investors are prepared to take more investment risk than others. This is true for investors in ETFs as well as individual stocks. It is certainly not a recommendation that you buy any high-flyers just for call option writing, because the large call option premiums sometimes available on such ETFs often don't outweigh the increased risk of owning such an ETF. Having said that, there are some pretty interesting returns a person can get writing call options on them if you own any.

OWNING AND WRITING CALLS ON HIGH RISK ETFs

On the next page is an example of how an investor could take advantage of an ETF with a high level of price volatility. The worksheet below shows covered call writing calculations on a hypothetical ETF called OOO Technology Fund, a sector fund. Since ETFs with significant price volatility have call options with large premiums, you would get a much higher total return by writing options on OOO Technology Fund than you could with an ETF having lower price volatility.

WRITING CALLS ON A HIGH RISK ETF

DATE ——>		6-Jul					
X	X	X		X	X	X	
CO.	#	SHARE	MARKET		OPTION		
SYM.	SHS.	PRICE	VALUE	DIV.	EXPIR.	STRIKE	DAYS
OOO	1,000	$50.00	$50,000	$0.00	17-Aug	$50.00	42
OOO	1,000	$50.00	$50,000	$0.00	19-Oct	$50.00	105
OOO	1,000	$50.00	$50,000	$0.00	18-Jan	$50.00	196
OOO	1,000	$50.00	$50,000	$0.00	18-Jan	$50.00	561
OOO	1,000	$50.00	$50,000	$0.00	17-Aug	$55.00	42
OOO	1,000	$50.00	$50,000	$0.00	19-Oct	$55.00	105
OOO	1,000	$50.00	$50,000	$0.00	18-Jan	$55.00	196
OOO	1,000	$50.00	$50,000	$0.00	18-Jan	$55.00	561
OOO	1,000	$50.00	$50,000	$0.00	17-Aug	$60.00	42
OOO	1,000	$50.00	$50,000	$0.00	19-Oct	$60.00	105
OOO	1,000	$50.00	$50,000	$0.00	18-Jan	$60.00	196
OOO	1,000	$50.00	$50,000	$0.00	18-Jan	$60.00	561

X	X	X						
			$	PREM.		TOTAL	MAX.	ANNUAL
CO.	OPTION		PREM.	$ PER	CONT.	ANNUAL	CAP.	YIELD W/
SYM.	SYMBOL	PREM.	INC.	DAY	YIELD	YIELD	APP.	CAP. APP.
OOO	OOOHJ	$2.85	$2,850	$67.86	5.70%	49.54%	$0	49.54%
OOO	OOOJJ	$4.65	$4,650	$44.29	9.30%	32.33%	$0	32.33%
OOO	OOOAJ	$6.45	$6,450	$32.91	12.90%	24.02%	$0	24.02%
OOO	VOOAJ	$11.30	$11,300	$20.14	22.60%	14.70%	$0	14.70%
OOO	OOOHK	$0.95	$950	$22.62	1.90%	16.51%	$5,000	103.42%
OOO	OOOJK	$2.35	$2,350	$22.38	4.70%	16.34%	$5,000	51.10%
OOO	OOOAK	$4.10	$4,100	$20.92	8.20%	15.27%	$5,000	33.89%
OOO	VOOAK	$9.00	$9,000	$16.04	18.00%	11.71%	$5,000	18.22%
OOO	OOOHL	$0.25	$250	$5.95	0.50%	4.35%	$10,000	178.15%
OOO	OOOJL	$1.10	$1,100	$10.48	2.20%	7.65%	$10,000	77.17%
OOO	OOOAL	$2.45	$2,450	$12.50	4.90%	9.13%	$10,000	46.37%
OOO	VOOAL	$7.25	$7,250	$12.92	14.50%	9.43%	$10,000	22.45%

You can see here that there are some big returns that can be had by writing call options on this ETF. If you write the $50 strike price, which is right at the current market price, you can get an annualized yield of over 49% on the very short-term option, to an annualized yield of almost 15% if you write the LEAPS expiring in January about 1 ½ years later

Even if you were to allow yourself quite a bit of extra room for capital appreciation by writing the $55 strike price option, your annualized yield would range from over 16% for the short-term call to almost 12% for the LEAPS expiring in January. The LEAPS at a strike price of $50 would give you $11.30 per share of downside protection and put a total of well over $11,000 in your pocket immediately, which could be reinvested now to produce more option writing income. Of course, there's always the possibility that it could skyrocket and you would have been better off just holding the ETF. That's the dilemma. This as an example of how high risk/high volatility ETFs pay large call premiums to the option writer. But, even though this can give you considerable downside protection, it obviously doesn't fully protect you if the ETF would tumble far downward.

BUYING ETFs ON MARGIN
AND WRITING COVERED CALLS

Another high risk strategy for the aggressive investor is buying ETFs on "margin." This is not a strategy to be employed by most investors, but for those willing to take higher risks it is possible that there may be a time when the outlook for option writing is so favorable that an aggressive investor would consider leveraging in order to obtain superior returns.

A margin account is a brokerage account component that has been pre-approved by the brokerage through a margin agreement to permit an investor to purchase securities on credit and to borrow on securities already in the account. Interest is charged at favorable rates on any borrowed funds during the time that the loan is in effect.

When you buy on margin you buy ETFs partially with your own money and partially with credit your broker provides. It's something like when you put a down payment on a house and then borrow the rest. Buying on margin generally allows you to buy up to twice as much of an ETF with the amount of money you have than if you just used your funds alone. If all goes well, you would have twice as much gain by using margin than without it, less the interest cost. The other side of the coin is that if the ETF goes down, you lose twice as much as you otherwise would have lost. So, there's both reward and risk. For people who are comfortable using debt to leverage ETF investments, the relatively low rate of interest you pay on the loan to the broker can be earned many times over if the ETF goes up and if you are regularly collecting option premiums. If it goes down, however, not only have you lost twice as much, but you are paying interest for the privilege.

The further risk is that if the market goes down considerably, you would at some point get a "**margin call**" from the broker to add more money or securities to your account, or they would need to sell you out...most likely at a loss. Obviously you would not want to do this unless you have a pretty constructive option writing outlook going forward.

For investors willing to assume more risk, it may potentially fit into an option writing strategy. By borrowing on margin to buy ETFs and then writing covered call options on twice as many shares of an ETF, it is possible in a flat to rising market to earn substantially more on your investment than if you just invested with your own funds. In a down market, it would be a disaster.

BROKERAGE ACCOUNTS AND
WRITING COVERED CALL OPTIONS

Now it is time to delve into the mechanics of how to make this all happen. As stated earlier, purchase/sale of ETFs and utilizing the covered call writing strategy can be done through either a discount broker or a full-service broker. If you have an investment advisor or broker who is performing miracles for you, then he/she may be worth the extra money you pay in commissions. If that is not the case, it is very difficult to beat the low cost and ease of use through online access of a discount broker. You are encouraged to review some of the discount brokers listed in the Appendix of this book and compare commission costs for ETF trades and option trades as well as compare services offered. Since you will be incurring additional commissions as a call writer, it is important to keep your commission costs down in order to maximize the opportunity to realize your investment return objective. The rest of this chapter operates under the assumption that you are trading through an online discount broker and utilize a cash management type of account.

In the event you do not have a computer and/or do not have an Internet access you will still be able to implement the strategies in this book. Please refer to the sections in the Appendix titled "How to Use a Discount Broker Without a Computer and Calculating Covered Call Writing Opportunities Manually" and "How to Manually Track Your Option Writing Transactions." It is more work than using a computer, but will become much easier with practice. Keep in mind that many public libraries today offer free high-speed Internet service, which can be used both to research ETFs as well as for doing your trading through a broker.

ONLINE DISCOUNT BROKERAGES

You need to do your option trading with the brokerage where you have your ETFs. Once you get the hang of it, trading ETFs and call options online is much quicker, easier and less expensive than dealing with humans. For example, it is very cumbersome to be going to a human broker to find out what option strike prices and expiration dates are offered for the ETFs you own so that you can make decisions on your writing program. You also need to obtain bid and ask quotes. Finally you need to place your orders and get quick feedback on whether your orders are filled. All of this information is available through an online broker as fast as you can make your fingers move on a keyboard and mouse. You really won't have any need to work with an individual unless you have some kind of problem with your account.

COMMISSIONS

The discount brokers generally charge far less than full-service brokerages, but even among the discounters there's a lot of difference. Most of all you want to be sure you are dealing with a substantial brokerage firm who will be around for at least as long as you are.

Typically discount brokerages charge for option trades based upon two components. First, there is usually a flat fee per transaction. This is why it is more cost efficient when you trade a larger number of call contracts, as this component doesn't change regardless of how many contracts are traded. Second, there is usually also a fee per option contract as well. This component tends to make it more expensive to trade a large number of option contracts on a lower priced ETF or with a small premium.

These two components are added together and charged as one fee per trade. As an example, let's say there is a $20 flat fee plus $1.75 per contract. If an investor sells 10 calls on an ETF, the commission would be $37.50. The larger the number of contracts traded, the smaller the commission as a percentage of the premium collected.

You can see that the way this fee schedule is structured, the commission does not vary with the amount of the premium collected. Therefore a commission schedule with a flat fee and per contract charge would tend to favor longer-term call options, as they will always have a larger premium per contract than a shorter-term option.

For example, let's look at what the commission situation would be if you wrote call option contracts on from 100 to 2,000 shares of an ETF using this commission schedule...that would be from one to twenty contracts. We'll look at it two ways...with a $1 premium per contract and with a $3 premium per contract.

	$1 PREMIUM				$3 PREMIUM		
# CONT.	PREM. INCOME	COMM.	COMM. %	# OF CONT.	PREM. INCOME	COMM.	COMM. %
1	$100	21.75	21.75%	1	$300	21.75	7.25%
2	$200	23.50	11.75%	2	$600	23.50	3.92%
3	$300	25.25	8.42%	3	$900	25.25	2.81%
4	$400	27.00	6.75%	4	$1,200	27.00	2.25%
5	$500	28.75	5.75%	5	$1,500	28.75	1.92%
6	$600	30.50	5.08%	6	$1,800	30.50	1.69%
7	$700	32.25	4.61%	7	$2,100	32.25	1.54%
8	$800	34.00	4.25%	8	$2,400	34.00	1.42%
9	$900	35.75	3.97%	9	$2,700	35.75	1.32%
10	$1,000	37.50	3.75%	10	$3,000	37.50	1.25%
11	$1,100	39.25	3.57%	11	$3,300	39.25	1.19%
12	$1,200	41.00	3.42%	12	$3,600	41.00	1.14%
13	$1,300	42.75	3.29%	13	$3,900	42.75	1.10%
14	$1,400	44.50	3.18%	14	$4,200	44.50	1.06%
15	$1,500	46.25	3.08%	15	$4,500	46.25	1.03%
16	$1,600	48.00	3.00%	16	$4,800	48.00	1.00%
17	$1,700	49.75	2.93%	17	$5,100	49.75	0.98%
18	$1,800	51.50	2.86%	18	$5,400	51.50	0.95%
19	$1,900	53.25	2.80%	19	$5,700	53.25	0.93%
20	$2,000	55.00	2.75%	20	$6,000	55.00	0.92%

You can see that the commissions paid are the same for both the $1 premium per contract and the $3 premium per contract. But the commission paid as a percentage of the premium income collected is only one-third as much for the options with a $3 premium as for those with a $1 premium.

Also, obviously longer-term options expire less frequently. A writer of options expiring in one month would need to trade three times more frequently than a writer of options expiring in three months. So, you pay a lesser percentage of the premium income in commissions by writing call options with longer-term expiration dates. Of course, the commissions paid is just one of many factors an investor would take into consideration as part of an overall option writing strategy.

Commissions on option trades tend to be higher than the discount brokerage commissions charged for an ETF purchase or sale, which often run between $10 and $30, depending on the broker. But in recent years, fees on options trades have come down significantly and represent only a very small percentage of the call option writing income you will be collecting. And you will become a very important client to your broker. As you write more and more call option contracts, they will collect more fee income from you than if you were just the casual ETF or stock trader. It should be a win/win situation for both you and the brokerage. You may be in a position to ask them for a favor or special service now and then. Maybe they will even give you a free trade on occasion.

There are many online brokers such as Accutrade, Ameritrade, CSFB Direct, Datek, E-Trade, TD Waterhouse, and on and on. Fidelity Investments and Charles Schwab & Company are often thought of first, as they are among the largest and most financially sound. The commissions are somewhat higher with Schwab and Fidelity than with some of the other online brokers, but they are much, much lower than traditional full-service brokers. They both offer a full-blown cash management account at no extra charge and they pay a market rate of interest on uninvested cash balances. An investor should be able to go to the Web site of any of the online brokerages and check out the fees for ETF/stock and option trades very easily. Or, a phone call could be made to get the same information.

The "calls" template on the diskette with this book can be easily customized to include all ETF and option fees charged by your brokerage into the return calculations. Just follow the instructions for use of the template in the Appendix and your calculations will be exact.

There's no difference in eligibility between writing covered calls in a personal and an IRA account as long as you are approved for option writing in both accounts by your brokerage.

There are two things important to focus on in conjunction with writing covered calls through your brokerage account. The first is getting the information you need to complete the Excel template so you can make your decisions on what calls to write. Second is the process of executing the option transactions. The rest of it takes care of itself. When you write covered calls your broker will credit the cash to our brokerage account the next day. All of the mechanics occur automatically. Not only will the cash be put into your brokerage account the next day, but with a cash management account they will automatically invest the cash in the money market fund you have selected for your account. That way your premium income is earning interest until you decide to withdraw it or to reinvest it in something else. And, if you have a margin loan balance, the money credited to your account from the premium income would automatically reduce the loan balance.

THE OPTION AGREEMENT

Before we focus on these two key points, there is one critical piece of paperwork that will need to be completed before any option writing can be done. You need to sign an

"Option Agreement" for each account you have with your brokerage so that you can trade covered call options. What you need to do is to call or write them, tell them that you want to write covered calls in your accounts, and ask them to send you the necessary paperwork to set up your accounts for options. They will send the Option Agreement form to fill out and also a publication they are required to provide called *Characteristics and Risks of Standardized Options*. This is a very informative booklet that reviews options terminology and theory, tells about the different kinds of options, how they can be used and the relative risks. As previously mentioned, some option strategies involve high risk and some, like covered call writing, are very conservative. This booklet reviews it all.

The purpose of the agreement is to help the brokerage assure that the investor has adequate knowledge about investing in options and that the option transactions are suitable for the investor. By the time you finish this book, you will be very knowledgeable about writing covered calls. But you should go ahead and request this now to get the account set up so you are ready.

The Option Agreement covers a wide variety of option strategies, so when you complete the paperwork you should only indicate that you want to write covered call options. You will also be asked about your investment knowledge and activity, and you should answer those questions honestly.

Finally, you will be asked about your investment objectives on the agreement. You should answer that you desire to produce income, which is consistent with writing covered calls.

Once you see the paperwork you'll find it easy to complete. Just answer the questions discussed here and return it to your broker. It should be approved in a few days and you will be ready to initiate trades.

COMPLETING THE WORKSHEET DATA

As you know, you need to fill in all of the columns that have an "x" at the top. Once you log on to your online brokerage account, you can find out the ticker symbol for any ETF. You probably would do that by clicking on the quote section of their Web page and then entering the name or ticker symbol of the ETF. The process is similar with Fidelity, Schwab and other online brokers. A little looking around for the right place to point and click should get you where you want to be. Of course, if there are any problems finding what you need, you can always call the brokerage firm directly and ask them a few questions until you are familiar with the process. After that it will become very automatic, because you will be using their Web pages frequently.

After you have entered the ETF name, ticker symbol, the number of shares and the dividend rate onto the Excel template, you are ready to get into the option writing part.

If you scroll to the right of the brokerage commission schedule columns on the Excel template you will see a progressive list of monthly option expiration dates. You should select the dates you want, one at a time, by placing your cursor over the first date, pressing the "Copy" button, and then placing the cursor in the appropriate cell under the "Option Expiration" column. Then press the "Paste" button and the date will be there. You should do that on a separate line for each option expiration date you want to consider. Then you need to type in the strike price you wish to review. Remember, you will almost always want to be working with call options that have a strike price somewhat above the current market price of your ETFs. You may need to create some more rows and replicate the information for the same ETF if you have a lot of expiration dates and strike prices you want to consider.

Once you have this information in the template, you are ready to begin looking up quotes. This may be done a bit differently with various online brokerages, but typically what you do is request a quote on the ETF by typing in the ticker symbol for the underlying ETF. When you have the ETF quote, you can then enter the current price information on the template in the appropriate column so it is up to date. When you are getting a quote on the ETF, you should find the words **"option chain"** somewhere near the quote. By clicking on this, their system should take you to a listing of all of the expiration dates and strike prices offered for the ETF. By scrolling up and down, you should be able to see the option ticker symbol for each option you wish to consider. As you scroll by them, note the ticker symbol for those you want and type in that information in the correct cell on the Excel template. Again, if it isn't obvious after a little searching how to find this, a call to the customer service center should get you the information you need. As an alternative, Yahoo! Finance also provides extensive options chains for stocks and ETFs.

After you have gotten this information for a given ETF and the call option you've selected, your row should be filled up to the premium column on the template. Now it's time to get the premium quotes on the option symbols and enter that information. By entering the option ticker symbol into the broker's online quotation inquiry system, the system should give you a number of pieces of information about the quote you are looking for.

Most importantly, it should give you the current bid and ask prices. That is even more important that the last price at which the option has traded. It may have been some time since the last option trade, and the underlying ETF has probably gone up or down. This would mean that the bid and ask for the option has also gone up or down, sometimes causing the last trade price to be out of date. Generally, when you are looking to do a trade on a call option, you can expect to make your trade at about the midpoint between the bid and ask, or perhaps a little bit closer toward the bid side. As mentioned previously, it is suggested that you add the bid and ask together, divide by two, and then place the resulting amount, or perhaps even slightly less, as the number in the premium column on the template.

After entering the option price, the rest of the data will complete itself automatically. By entering the quotes in this way for each option symbol onto the template, you are then in a position to take a look at the worksheet and make a decision on what option you wish to write.

That is how you use your online quotation system to obtain the information you need to complete your template. Gathering all of this data may take awhile initially, but it will go quickly and smoothly after you have done it a few times. Now you can make your investment decisions.

We won't discuss the decision making process again, as this was discussed in detail earlier. Of course your goal is to achieve your total return objective while obtaining diversity in your option expiration dates and basing your strike price decisions on how you think the ETF will be performing between now and the time the option that you are considering will expire.

In deciding which contract to write, remember there is no assurance that your ETF will rise to the strike price at expiration, which is reflected in the "Annual Yield With Capital Appreciation" column. Therefore, the most realistic and conservative way to evaluate this would be to look primarily at the "Total Annual Yield" for your decisions. Then you should balance out all of your decisions to reach your target yield return. That way you can consider the capital appreciation as "icing on the cake" if it happens.

ONLINE COVERED CALL OPTION TRADING

So, after considering the alternatives, you've made a decision on a call option to write. At this point you are now ready to use the online brokerage to execute the option transaction. What you need to do now when you are logged on to your brokerage account is to go to the Web page online that is used for option trades.

Now go back to the first worksheet showing the calculations for the six ETFs. Let's assume that you are going to execute the trade in the second row on the printout for BBB...namely, you are going to write 30 contracts of the October $20 calls. The option symbol is BBBJD and the current quote midpoint is $1.30.

The information required by different brokers for their online system should be essentially the same. The pieces of it may just be located in different places on their Web pages. You will become familiar with your broker's pages very quickly after you do a few option trades.

There should appear several choices for the kind of option trade you wish to place. The buyer of an option would click on "buy" to purchase a call option or "sell" in order to sell it. As you are not a buyer, but are a writer of call options, to initiate a new transaction you will always click on "sell-to-open" or "sell covered call," however it is termed by your brokerage. You are selling...that is, writing...the option, and the transaction is an opening transaction. You will enter the number of contracts, remembering that one option contract is for one hundred shares of the underlying ETF. In this example you would enter 30. You then need to type in the option symbol in the appropriate place to be sure you get the right contract. Get this information from your template.

There will also be a section that will ask you to click whether you wish a **"market order"** or a **"limit order."** A limit order requires that a **"limit price"** be set.

If you select market order, the transaction will be carried out at the "best price available" when the order reaches the marketplace. It assures that the transaction will be executed at some price. The difficulty with options sometimes is that they are not as liquid as the underlying ETF. The ETF BBB, for example, trades millions of shares per day, but there are not millions of call options for BBB that trade daily. The number of option contracts traded in a day is much, much smaller. As a result, even though there is a highly efficient, fungible market for options, sometimes the difference between the bid and ask can be wide and can change to an investor's disadvantage if a market order is placed. You could then end up getting your order filled for something less than the price you were expecting. For that reason, it is suggested that you *always use limit orders and set a limit price* for your option trades. While you will not be guaranteed that your order will be filled, you will be assured that if it *is* filled the price you will receive will not be less than the limit price you have set...and it may be more, depending on the best price available at the time.

So, you should click on "limit order" and then set a limit price you are willing to accept. Since your transaction will not be completed for less than the limit price, you need to be sure that the amount you set is either at the midpoint between the bid and ask or perhaps even a bit lower to give greater assurance that the transaction will be completed. For example, if the bid on your option transaction is $1.10

and the ask is $1.50, to have a reasonable assurance that your order will get filled, you should bid about $1.30. Or, you could plug $1.20 into your calculation template, and if that amount would result in a return that is acceptable, you could consider entering your limit order for $1.20.

The risk is that if you enter a market order you will often get filled at the bottom end, namely the bid of $1.10 in this case, or even lower on occasion. By setting a realistic limit order price, you can almost always get your transaction completed and assure yourself that you are getting a reasonable market price for your option trades.

If you were to put in a limit price that is a bit higher than the midpoint between the bid and ask, it would probably take a rise in the price of the underlying ETF and correspondingly the option, before your trade would be executed. Since there would be no assurance that the price would go up, your order might not be filled.

There is one risk you do run, however, when setting a limit price. If by the time you get your order placed the price of the underlying ETF has declined, then the option price will have also declined and your order will not be filled unless the price of the ETF and the option rise again. The best guard against this is to be sure you have a very current quote on the bid and ask for the option contract and that you enter your limit order as quickly as possible after you have made your decision to write the option. In the event the price of the ETF declines, however, you should be prepared to cancel your option order and replace it with a lower limit price. Otherwise you would need to wait to see if the market recovers to your price. You can see that much of this would be difficult if you were dealing with a live broker and had to be making phone calls back and forth until your trades were completed.

Of course, if the bid price fulfills your return objective and is acceptable to you, you could actually enter the bid amount as your price, but you should typically try to do at least somewhat better than that. You can plug in quotes for various premium alternatives into your template to see what the yields look like compared with your objective.

There's another element that needs to be mentioned...an "all-or-none order."

When initiating an option trade, "all or none" is a further restricting element of a limit order whereby you specify that either your entire order be executed at the same time or none of it is to be executed. For example, if you are trying to sell-to-open ten call contracts, it is possible that only part of your order might be filled...say two contracts, with the order for the other eight not filled if the price of the option should quickly back off of your limit price. If you have to go in later and alter your price to fill the rest of your order, or if the balance of your limit order is not filled until a later date, your commission costs would go up. These trades would be treated as separate transactions for commission purposes.

The "all or none order" is a good idea, particularly when you are dealing with options that are thinly traded. It's not always possible to know how liquid the market is for the options you are trading. As you gain more experience with option trading you will get a feel for this. You should also be able to get volume information on option contracts from your broker's quotation system. At least initially it may be advisable for you to use "all or none" orders to avoid partial order fills. When you are initiating your transaction, either online or through an automated voice response phone system, you will be asked whether you wish to place any special conditions on the transaction. This will give you an opportunity to indicate if you wish the order to be "all or none."

There's one final element to add. You also have an opportunity to indicate the time-in-force of the transaction. You can specify that the order will only be valid for the day, referred to as a **"day order,"** or that it will be a **"good-'til-canceled order,"** also referred to as **"GTC."** This would be entirely up to you. If you use orders that are valid only for the day and the order is not filled, that provides an opportunity to reevaluate what you want to do at that point. You can then enter a new order for the following day. With a good-'til-canceled order, the order will remain on the brokerages books until it is filled or until the order time limit expires.

The process of trading options is pretty much the same as trading stocks or ETFs. Since you are looking up quite a few quotes, computing a midpoint between bid and ask, and entering the information into the template for review, it may just seem a bit more complicated at first. It is more work with options, but the end result definitely justifies it. And the more trades you do, the easier it will get.

Once you have entered your order, you can check your online account at any time to see if the order is still pending or if it has been executed. Until it is filled, you will probably want to continue to monitor the price of the underlying ETF and the option to see if you need to make any adjustment to your limit price if the market declines. Or you may wish to wait it out to see if the market recovers to your price.

In addition to receiving a brokerage statement periodically in the mail, you can, of course, also check at any time online to see a current statement of positions and cash balances as well as a transaction history. When you have written covered calls, the calls will show up online and on your brokerage statements as a negative balance until the options expire or are assigned. This is a "**short position**" offset to the cash you received into your account. It will reflect the current market price of the options as they fluctuate up and down based upon the price of the underlying ETF. In addition to the price of the underlying ETF, the other variable that will affect the price of the option is the time remaining until expiration. If the price of the ETF were to remain constant after the trade, the negative balance of the option on your brokerage statement would eventually diminish to zero as time dwindles to the expiration date.

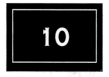

TRACKING RESULTS

Now that you are ready to start your option writing program it's important that you have a mechanism to keep track of how you are doing on an ongoing basis compared with your objective. To accomplish that, another template using Excel is included on the diskette at the back of the book...a file called "results." There is also an instruction page in the Appendix outlining exactly what data to enter into the template. Worksheets are included at the end of the book for use by those who are not using a computer.

On the next page is a sample of how you would use this file template.

RESULTS TRACKING TEMPLATE

SORTED BY TRADE

X	X	X	X		X	X	X		X	X	X	X		
				MARKET	TRADE				OPTION		PREM.	STOCK	$	%
ACCT.	STOCK	SHS.	COST	VALUE	DATE	EXPIR.	STRIKE	DAYS	SYMBOL	PREM.	INC.	GAIN/LOSS	RETURN	RETURN
PER	BBB	3,000	$18.00	$54,060	1-Jul-00	19-Oct-00	$20.00	110	BBBJD	$1.35	$4,007	$0	$4,007	24.60%
IRA	KKK	1,000	$48.90	$48,920	5-Jul-00	21-Dec-00	$50.00	169	KKKLJ	$2.95	$2,913	$1,100	$4,013	17.71%
											$6,920	$1,100		

The appearance is reminiscent of the "calls" file, but serves a different purpose. Again, the "x" at the top in some of the columns means you need to type in that information. Otherwise the template makes the calculations. There are a few more columns with an "x" in this template. To start you need to enter the account type in the first column. This is particularly handy, as we'll see in a minute, if you have more than one account. You may wish to enter "PER" in this column for transactions having to do with your taxable personal account and "IRA" for an IRA account. You can obviously use whatever designation you wish, as long as you are consistent. If you have only one brokerage account, you could leave this column blank. In the column before the expiration date, you enter the date of the trade. If, for example, the trade date was August 15, 2001, you would type 8/15/2001 into the cell. You also need to enter the net amount of the premium income as shown in your brokerage confirmation. Also, if your ETF is called away from you or otherwise sold, you need to determine the gain or loss on the ETF (the amount of capital appreciation or capital depreciation realized based upon the price of the ETF on the date when the calls were written) and enter that information in total dollars as well. That's all there is to it. In the unusual circumstance that you bought back your call options prior to expiration, you would need to reduce the amount of premium income you received by the amount you paid to buy back the options.

You can see in the first example that this option writer wrote 30 call contracts of the BBB October $20 calls in a personal taxable account and received $4,007 in premium income. As the option expired unexercised, there was no sale of the ETF and therefore no gain or loss. The annualized percentage return was 24.60%. In the second example, the option writer wrote 10 call contracts of the KKK December $50 calls and received $2,913. At expiration the ETF was priced above $50, so the ETF was called away. The investor's gain on the ETF during the period of this trade was $1,100. In this case, the dollar return column shows the combined premium income and gain on the ETF of $4,013 for a total annualized percentage return on the premium income and capital appreciation on the ETF of 17.71%.

You will see that at the top left hand corner of the worksheet it says "Sorted By Trade." Excel has a sorting capability that can be used to your advantage with this template. You will see on your computer screen at the bottom left of the worksheet on the template itself that there are four tabs labeled "Trade Sort," "Expiration Sort," "ETF Sort" and "Account Sort." The "Trade Sort" template is the one we've been talking about so far, and it should be used as your primary results template for entering data. The others are available for your use if you decide it is important for you to be able to look at your results information sorted by expiration date, or by ETF, or by account. Obviously the last one would only apply if you have more than one brokerage account where you are writing options.

The best time to enter the information into the "Trade Sort" template is when you get your broker confirmations in the mail and when options expire. Or, you can get the information online after the trade is executed. Here's what to do if you want to use the other sorting methods. Start by going to the "Trade Sort" template and highlight all of the data by placing the cursor in the upper left hand cell where your data starts. Click on your mouse button while holding it down and drag the cursor to the right and down until it darkens all of the data cells on your worksheet. Then let go of the mouse button and all of your data will be selected. Now click on the "Copy" icon at the top and then click on the tab at the bottom you wish to use. It will take you to that tab, which has the same appearance as the worksheet you see here. Point and click the cursor into the same cell address as the cell from which you started copying the data. Then all you have to do is click on the "Paste" icon and all of the data you copied will be pasted into the new worksheet. The tabbed worksheets have been formatted so that they will sort according to what the tab says. So all you need to do now is keep the data highlighted and then click on the word "Data" at the top. A drop down menu box will appear. Click on "Sort" and another drop down menu comes up. Just click on the "OK" box at the bottom and your data is sorted.

It can be useful to look at your data by ETF, for example, so that you can see how many times you have written options on a specific ETF and how it has worked out for you. That will give you a very good feel for the market over time. You can also enter data into the other tabs and sort by expiration date or by account type.

TAX CONSEQUENCES OF
COVERED CALL WRITING

People always say they wish they had a big tax problem...until they actually have one, that is, and then they want to wish it gone. When you have success with a call option writing strategy in a personal account it's going to mean more income taxes to pay. But, on the other hand, you are going to have a lot more income than you otherwise would have had, so that obviously more than makes up for it.

TAXABLE ACCOUNTS

As we've said earlier, when you write call options you get the premium income up front into your account the next day to use as you wish. The good news from a tax standpoint is that *even though you have the use of the premium income immediately, it isn't taxed to you until the options expire* or until you close out your position if you buy-to-close, whichever occurs first. That can lead to some tax planning opportunities at times, depending on the time of year and the expiration date on the options you are writing.

Let's say that you wrote options on KKK with a July expiration date and the options expired without your ETF being called away. Now you are ready to write another option. You look at the premiums that are available for various expiration dates. You also look at your tax picture and realize that you have built up a lot of taxable income during this tax year and you would like to try to defer some taxable income into the next tax year. What you could do is to select one of the call options with an expiration in January or later of next year. That way the premium income you receive on those options now will not be taxed to you until the options expire, which would be in the next tax year. You have just deferred the income tax consequence into next year, even though you have the money right now. And you can do this with as many different ETFs and options contracts as you like. This can give you a pretty powerful tax planning tool at times.

Speaking of tax consequences, perhaps the most important point is that the premium income you receive from writing calls is "**capital gain**" for tax purposes. The bad news is that the premiums are almost always "**short-term**" capital gain regardless of the length of time the call was outstanding. That means your option writing income is usually taxed at the same rate as if it were "**ordinary income.**" You will need to report your option trades on Schedule D of Form 1040.

And, if you would decide to close out your option position by buying back the options, any gain or loss would be short-term capital gain or loss in the year that the position was closed out. For example, let's say you wrote options in July that were not due to expire until the following year and you received $3,000 in premium income. In November you bought back the options for $1,000. You would have a short-term capital gain of $2,000 for the tax year in which you bought back the options, not in the next tax year when the options would have otherwise expired.

CAPITAL GAIN VS. CAPITAL APPRECIATION

We've used the term "capital appreciation" frequently so far, and now we are referring to "capital gain." There is an important difference. When we are talking about capital appreciation, it is an investment term that simply means an increase in value of a security, such as an ETF or an option. For example, if an ETF goes from $35 to $50, it has experienced capital appreciation of $15 per share. Capital gain is a tax term that comes into play only when a capital asset, such as an ETF or option, is sold. It occurs when the proceeds from the sale of an ETF or an option is greater than its cost.

You are likely aware that if you have capital gains you can offset them with capital losses to reduce your tax burden. So, if you had an ETF you took a **"capital loss"** on, you could use that loss to offset some of the gains you realize on your option writing income. If you had some gains from writing call options, you could also use prior year losses carried forward to offset the gains on the option income. And for any current **"unrealized loss"** in any of your ETFs, you could sell those ETFs and use the realized capital losses to offset option writing income.

AN EXCEPTION: WHEN SHORT-TERM CAPITAL GAIN FROM CALL WRITING CAN BE TREATED AS LONG-TERM GAIN

The tax effect may be different, and beneficial to you, if your calls are assigned and your ETF is sold to the option holder at expiration. If you sell calls and the calls are assigned, the strike price at which you sell your ETF *plus* the premium you received becomes the sale price of the ETF to determine the amount of gain or loss. Let's say you had paid $20 per share several years ago for your ETF. The ETF was trading at $42, and you had written call options on it for a premium of $2 per share at a strike price of $45. On expiration the ETF was called away from you at the strike price. Your gain would be $45 minus $20 plus $2, or $27 per share. When your ETF is assigned, the resulting gain or loss depends upon the cost of the underlying ETF delivered and the holding period of the ETF. What is meant by "holding period" is the length of time you have owned the ETF. In this case, because you had held the ETF for a long enough time period to have it qualify for **"long-term"** capital gain treatment, the gain on your ETF *and the option premium* will be long-term capital gain at a favorable tax rate. So, this is the exception when an option premium is taxed as a long-term capital gain rather than a short-term capital gain.

Here's the rule. Writing an at-the-money or an out-of-the-money covered call does not affect the holding period of the underlying ETF for purposes of determining whether any gain is long-term or short-term if the ETF is eventually assigned. This will cover almost all of the transactions you will be doing. The tax consequences on in-the-money transactions can sometimes become more complicated too, especially if the underlying ETF would qualify as a long-term holding for tax purposes. It is unlikely that you would be doing any such transaction, but you should consult your tax advisor if you did. And there's always talk about possible changes in the tax rates for capital gains based on the holding period, so it's a good idea to keep up with that or to consult your tax advisor.

Earlier buying ETFs on margin and writing options on them was discussed. If you did that, and if you itemize deductions on your tax returns, you should be able to take the investment interest expense as an itemized deduction up to the combined amount of any interest income and dividend income you report on your tax return. Remember, the premium income from option writing is capital gain, not interest income. If your investment interest expense exceeds your combined interest and dividend income, then the excess interest expense can be carried over as a deduction to the following tax year.

It's always a good idea to consult your tax advisor about all of these tax matters. The laws are cumbersome and they can always change.

THE CHALLENGE OF WRITING CALLS ON HIGHLY APPRECIATED ETFs

As Ben Franklin said many years ago, there are only two certainties in life...death and taxes. We all generally accept this, but we'd like to be able to plan for both of them. As far as capital gains tax is concerned, we are used to having the certainty of timing it so that our best tax interests are served. When we are writing covered calls on ETFs we own that have grown in value substantially, we never know exactly when that big capital gain might be triggered through an exercise of the option causing a sale of the ETF.

First, you should never write a call option on an ETF that you are absolutely unwilling to sell. But the opportunity to earn call option premium income may outweigh the possibility that the ETF might be called away, triggering an unwanted capital gain. One choice might be to write calls on only a portion of the ETF. If it is called away, you would only have a portion of the total gain taxed to you. That way if the ETF price went up you could write options on the rest of the ETF at a higher strike price and structure it so the expiration date falls into the next tax year to spread out the potential tax on the gains if the rest of the ETF is called away.

Also, keep in mind that there are favorable tax laws for long-term capital gains on the sale of stocks, including ETFs. Under current law, for taxpayers in higher brackets, you would pay a lot less on the capital gain than you would on your ordinary income. Perhaps that's not much consolation if you are facing taxes on a big gain, but unless you donate the ETF to a charity or die owning it, taxes on the gain will be paid by someone at some point. Also Congress has been known to change the tax laws with some regularity. While we would hope any changes would be in our favor, there's no assurance that the tax on capital gains won't be greater at some point in the future than it is today.

But if you really don't want to trigger the capital gain, and you really do want to write options on the ETF, what can an investor do?

Let's assume that you have written calls on an ETF with a large unrealized long-term capital gain and that the price of this ETF has gone up above the strike price of the calls you have written. As we discussed before, options are usually not exercised until expiration, even though the buyer of the option has the right to exercise them at any time up through the expiration date. So, if you are, say, well within a month of expiration, and the price of the ETF is above the strike price of the calls, this is what you may wish to consider doing. In this case it may be advantageous to act before the expiration date. You can buy back the call contracts at the current market price to close out your option position, and then write new calls with a different and more distant expiration date.

This, in effect, would dispose of the old call option and defer the exercise of the new call option until a later date. If the new options have the same strike price as the old ones, the option premium on the new calls will always be greater than your cost in buying back the old calls. You could, of course, have a gain or loss on the old options when you buy them back. It would largely depend on how much the market value of the ETF went above the strike price of the original calls...in other words, how much intrinsic value there is.

There is a name for this. Buying back your calls and then writing new calls at the same strike price, but with a more distant expiration is called **"rolling forward."**

Let's say, for example, you bought shares of AAA ETF ten years ago. You now own 1,000 shares and your cost basis, adjusted for several splits, is only $5 per share. About 2 ½ months ago the market value of the ETF was $50 per share, or $50,000 worth of the ETF. At that time you sold ten call contracts on your AAA shares at a strike price of $55. Since then two months have passed and the options expire about two weeks from now.

When you wrote the options you collected a premium of $2.50 per share for total premium income of $2,500. From the date you wrote the options 2 ½ months ago the price of the ETF has gone from $50 to its current price of $57 per share. The call contracts you wrote are now priced at $3.50 reflecting the current intrinsic value of $2 per share (the $57 current market value less the $55 strike price) and the remaining time value of $1.50 per share (the $3.50 current market less the $2 intrinsic value). If you hold your position where it is now, and the price of the ETF remains above $55, you will realize a capital gain of $50 per share (the $55 strike price less your $5 cost basis) or $50,000 when the ETF is called away from you.

Not wanting to pay the capital gains taxes at this time, you decide that rolling forward is a strategy that makes sense for you. You get quotes from your broker on calls with the same strike price, but with a longer expiration date. There are several option expiration dates available to you.

Which one you select is purely a matter of preference and planning. You might want to take into consideration the expiration dates of calls currently existing that you have written on other ETFs for purposes of expiration diversification. After review, you decide on the contract at the same strike price and with an expiration date in about 6 ½ months. If your ETF were called away at this new expiration date, it would place the capital gain into the next tax year, which would be more acceptable to you. Of course, it's always possible that the ETF price may decline below the $55 strike price by the new expiration date, in which case you would keep your ETF and the new option premium income. There would be no capital gain realized on the ETF and therefore no taxes to pay in that event...just tax to pay on the short-term capital gain from the premium income.

The price of the option contract with the new expiration date is $5.50 (larger due to the longer expiration term). You are ready to roll forward.

First you buy back the old option contracts at $3.50 with an order to buy to close ten contracts. After the order is filled, you then sell-to-open (also termed "sell covered call ") ten contracts of the new option at $5.50. When that order is filled, you watch what happens until the new option expiration date approaches.

This sounds a lot more complicated than it really is. Let's first consider the sale and repurchase of the first option. You sold the initial calls for $2,500 and repurchased them for $3,500 for a loss of $1,000. This loss can be used to offset other capital gains you've earned. The new option transaction stands on its own. If held until expiration, the premium income of $5,500 would be taxed the same as other option transactions we've previously discussed. Of course, if the ETF is called away at the new option's expiration you would still have a $50,000 long-term capital gain to pay tax on.

What you have accomplished is that you have bought additional time and thereby have extended out the realization of the capital gain and the corresponding tax on it. And, again, if the ETF were to go back down below the strike price at expiration, the capital gain tax would be a moot issue.

If the price of the ETF just kept going up, there are a couple of choices you would have. First, you could just continue to roll forward the expiration dates by buying back the older contracts and writing new options as each expiration date approaches, just as we did in this example. The higher the price rises, however, the more likely it becomes that your ETF will eventually be called away from you at the $55 strike price at some point. So, if your ETF keeps rising, this strategy is simply one of deferral of the capital gain recognition to a time when it may be more acceptable from a tax planning standpoint than the present.

Going back to the example, another alternative would be to buy back the first call options and then write new calls with a higher strike price. This is referred to as "rolling up." Doing this can take the pressure off a bit, because if the strike price on the new option was $60, for example, you now have out-of-the-money calls that wouldn't be exercised at expiration unless the ETF continued to rise. If it did go up further, your ETF would be called away at $60, not $55, and you would have a $55,000 capital gain subject to tax.

Of course, the premium you would receive on a call with a $60 strike price would be quite a bit less than one with a $55 strike price. As you know, the higher the strike price for a call option, the lower the premium. Depending on how much higher the strike price is on the new option compared to the old option, and also how much further out the expiration is extended, the premium income on the new calls could be significantly reduced. You would have to consider all of the choices. The best alternative in some cases might be a combination of rolling forward and rolling up. A lot depends on what is going to happen later. Unfortunately, of course, we can't predict the future.

There is one additional alternative you should know about. It's not likely that you would use it often, if ever. But in a situation like this you might consider it. When you write calls on your ETF and your ETF is assigned, that doesn't mean that you have to deliver exactly those same shares. Like option contracts, shares of ETFs are fungible. That is to say, shares are freely interchangeable among investors. The buyer of your ETF subject to the calls doesn't care whether you deliver the shares you owned at the time your calls were written or different shares. Their fungibility makes them all the same. Therefore, if you would prefer not to deliver the shares you own, you can always purchase new shares on the open market and deliver them to fulfill your assignment obligation in place of the original shares you own. This would create an immediate capital loss rather than triggering the capital gain that would be realized by selling your original shares (as the market price you pay for these new shares would be higher than the strike price you are paid for the shares), but that might also work to your advantage, depending on your tax situation. You would, of course, need available cash or margin borrowing capability to buy these new shares to do this.

You can see why it is always best to write options on ETFs that you don't mind being called away from you at expiration. You just let the ETF be called away and accept your gains rather than having to chase a rising ETF by rolling forward and/or rolling up. Nonetheless, these are workable ways to handle the writing of call options on a highly appreciated ETF when the price of the ETF rises. It's best to have a plan at the very start so that if the ETF price increases significantly you know pretty well in advance what action you will want to take. As stated earlier, about eighty-percent of options that are out-of-the-money when written expire unexercised, so this scenario is not something you would frequently have to face...but forewarned is forearmed!

TAX DEFERRED ACCOUNTS

The best news is that none of these tax consequences apply when you are dealing with a tax-deferred account, such as an IRA, since no income or gain is taxed until actual distributions are made from the account. That gives an investor a tremendous opportunity to earn a large amount of current premium income and not pay any taxes on it until withdrawals are made from the account.

CONCLUSION

12

It has been over three decades since fungible options were first offered on regulated exchanges in the United States. There are a wide variety of strategies that can be employed using options...some highly risky, some conservative, and some in between. Perhaps it is because of the variety of alternatives investors have with the uses of options that the average investor remains largely confused and unaware of the use of options. In particular it is amazing that the most conservative option strategy of all...writing covered calls on stocks and Exchange Traded Funds...remains a mystery to the masses while its fruits are enjoyed primarily by the large institutional investors who manage billions and billions of dollars for themselves and for others.

There is evidence that the word is starting to get out to individual investors about covered call writing. Articles are appearing in magazines, guests are invited to speak on CNBC TV (the cable stock market channel) on the subject, and Web sites are being created offering outlandish claims of investment success.

Clearly the market doldrums have taken their toll on individual investors as they frantically seek out alternatives to "traditional" investing, having lost billions of dollars in the value of their stocks in recent years. Moreover, hearing from some of the country's best known and most respected investors, economists, and educators that future stock market returns may be paltry in the future when compared with the past for perhaps one or more decades to come is most unsettling for those who were looking forward to early retirement, or even normal retirement, especially for the huge number of so-called baby boomers.

Few good new investment ideas are apparent. While writing covered call options is certainly not new, it is new to most individual investors. If the flat to slow-growth market predictions of Warren Buffett, John Templeton, Jeremy Segal, Douglas Cliggott, Barton Biggs, John Bollinger, and many other knowledgeable professionals holds up, it would appear that the returns achievable from writing covered calls on individual stocks and ETFs may well be one of the few ways, if not the only way, to achieve double-digit investment returns for many years to come.

ALL-OR-NONE ORDER – A type of limit order which directs a broker to either fill the entire order or, if it cannot be filled, to fill none of it.

ASK – The price offered by an owner to sell a security, such as an ETF or an option.

ASSIGNED – The requirement by the writer of an option to perform according to the terms of the contract by making delivery of the underlying ETF to the holder (buyer) of the option. This is done by the option writer's broker.

AT-THE-MONEY – The strike price and the market price of the underlying ETF are exactly equal.

BID – The price offered by a buyer to purchase a security, such as an ETF or option.

BUY TO CLOSE – The placing of an order by an option writer to buy back the option in order to close out the position.

CALL – An option permitting the holder (buyer) to purchase an ETF at a predetermined price until a certain date. For example, an investor may purchase a call option on AAA ETF giving the investor the right to buy 100 shares (for each option contract) at $50 per share until June 15.

CAPITAL APPRECIATION – An increase in the market value of a security.

CAPITAL DEPRECIATION – A decrease in the market value of a security.

CAPITAL GAIN – Occurs when the proceeds from an ETF or an option sale is greater than its cost. When writing covered calls, for example, if you receive $3 per share in premium income and the calls expire worthless, your cost is $0 per share and the capital gain is $3 per share.

CAPITAL LOSS – Occurs when the proceeds from an ETF or an option sale is less than its cost. When writing covered calls, for example, if you receive $3 per share in premium income and you buy back the calls at $4, the capital loss is $1 per share.

COVERED – Implies that the investor who writes a call option owns the underlying ETF, so that if the ETF is assigned the writer has the ETF to deliver to the call holder (buyer).

COVERED CALL OPTION WRITING – An investment program for ETF owners and shareholders of individual companies who are generally seeking a conservative way to increase income from their shares by selling (writing) calls on the ETF they own. There is also the opportunity for a defined amount of capital appreciation in the ETF (for out-of-the-money calls) and the ETF owner receives any dividends. The option writer receives premium income in exchange for assuring that the buyer of the option can purchase the shares at the agreed strike price during the operative time period of the option contract.

CREATION UNIT –ETFs typically issue shares in creation unit size, from 25,000 to 600,000 shares, in exchange for a predefined basket of the underlying index securities.

DAY ORDER – An order to buy or sell a security that will expire at the end of the day the order is placed if it is not executed.

DOLLAR COST AVERAGING – Investment of money at regular or periodic intervals. This results in purchasing more shares during a down market and fewer shares during a rising market. Those who use dollar cost averaging believe that the price of the security they are purchasing will rise over the long term, but that it is not possible to know exactly when to buy it at the best price all at once.

EXCHANGE TRADED FUND (ETF) - ETFs represent shares of ownership in portfolios of common stocks which are designed to generally correspond to the price and yield performance of their underlying portfolios of securities, either broad market, industry sectors, regions, investment styles, or international. ETFs give investors the opportunity to buy or sell an entire portfolio of stocks within a single security, as easily as buying or selling a share of stock. They offer a wide range of investment opportunities.

EXERCISE – In the case of covered call options, to require delivery of the underlying ETF by the seller (writer) of the options to the holder (buyer).

EXPIRATION DATE – The last day an option holder (buyer) can exercise the rights in an option contract.

FUNGIBLE – Relates to assets that are identical and are interchangeable. For example, shares of QQQ, the Nasdaq-100 Index Tracking ETF or the April $35 QQQ calls are both fungible. All QQQ shares are the same and are interchangeable and all of the QQQ April $35 call contracts are the same and are interchangeable.

GOOD-"TIL-CANCELED ORDER (GTC) – An order to buy or sell a security that remains in force until it is executed or canceled.

INSTITUTIONAL INVESTOR – Large investors in the securities markets such as mutual funds, bank trust departments, insurance companies, brokerage firms and pension funds. Many institutional investors use covered call writing as one of their investment strategies.

IN-THE-MONEY – The strike price of a call option is below the market price of the underlying ETF. For example, the call option for an ETF with a strike price of $50 when the ETF is trading at $52 would be $2 in-the-money.

INTRINSIC VALUE – That part of an option's market price which is in-the-money. For example, if the current market price of an option is $3 ½ and the option is in-the-money by $2, the intrinsic value is $2 and the time value is $1 ½. If an option is at-the-money or out-of-the-money there is no intrinsic value.

LEAPS – An acronym for Long-Term Equity Anticipation Securities. These are options with expiration dates extending up to three years, which is well beyond the term of regular options.

LEVERAGE – An attempt by an investor to increase the rate of return from an investment by assuming additional risk. Examples of leverage would be buying securities on margin and speculating by purchasing options.

LIMIT ORDER – An order to execute a transaction only at a specified limit price or better. Investors would use a limit order to establish a price at which they are willing to trade.

LIMIT PRICE – The price specified by an investor for a limit order. For an order to write covered calls, this represents the lowest price the investor will accept.

LONG-TERM – Relates to the gain or loss in a security that has been held for a certain period of time. For example, to qualify as a long-term capital gain under current tax laws, a security must be held for twelve months or more.

MARGIN (ACCOUNT) – A feature of a brokerage account which permits an investor to borrow funds through the broker to purchase additional securities, thus providing investment leverage.

MARGIN CALL - A call by the broker for additional funds or securities to be added to the margin account when the value of the equity in the account has declined below minimum requirements.

MARKET ORDER - An order for immediate execution at the best price available when the order reaches the exchange.

ODD LOT - Refers to fewer than 100 shares of a common stock or ETF.

OPEN INTEREST - The total number of option contracts for an ETF option that are in existence at any given time.

OPTION - A contract permitting the holder (buyer) to purchase (call) or sell (put) an ETF at a fixed price (strike) until a specific date (expiration).

OPTION AGREEMENT - A written document that must be signed by an option investor and given to the brokerage firm before the investor may be approved for trading in options. The purpose of the agreement is to help assure that the investor has adequate knowledge (such as the knowledge contained in this book in the case of covered calls) and that the investor's goals are appropriate for the type of option transactions the investor is asking the brokerage firm to provide. The investor is also supplied with a copy of *Characteristics and Risks of Standardized Options*.

OPTION CHAIN - A string of option quotes for a specific ETF which includes every expiration date and strike price available for options on that ETF. This is typically provided by online brokers as a part of their automated quotation service to simplify the identification of ticker symbols for options and to facilitate obtaining quotes and executing trades.

OPTION CONTRACT – An agreement by an option writer to sell a given ETF at a predetermined price (strike) until a certain date (expiration). The holder (buyer) of the option is not obligated to exercise (act on) the option, but the seller (writer) of the option must perform the obligation if the buyer exercises rights under the option contract.

OPTION CYCLE – Each ETF is given a series of up to four months during which option contracts expire. Options for an ETF generally expire on the same four months every year, plus the current month and the next following month.

OPTIONS CLEARING CORPORATION – Referred to as the OCC, it is an organization established in 1972 to process and guarantee options transactions that take place on the organized exchanges.

ORDINARY INCOME – Income from sources such as wages, dividends and interest. These items of income do not qualify for special tax treatment. Short-term capital gains are also taxed as ordinary income.

OUT-OF-THE-MONEY - The strike price of a call option is above the market price of the underlying ETF. For example, the call option for an ETF with a strike price of $55 when the ETF is trading at $52 would be $3 out-of-the-money.

PREMIUM – The current price at which an option contract trades and the amount a buyer would pay and a seller would receive. The amount of the premium is determined by a variety of factors, including the time remaining to expiration, the strike price chosen, the price and volatility of the underlying ETF, and interest rates.

PUT - An option permitting the holder (buyer) to sell an ETF at a predetermined price until a certain date. For example, an investor may purchase a put option on AAA ETF giving the investor the right to sell 100 shares (for each option contract) at $50 per share until June 15.

ROLLING DOWN – Buying back a call option position and then writing a new call with the same maturity, but with a lower strike price.

ROLLING FORWARD – Buying back a call option position and then writing a new call at the same strike price, but with a longer expiration.

ROLLING UP – Buying back a call option position and then writing a new call with the same maturity, but with a higher strike price.

ROUND LOT – For common stocks and ETFs the standard unit of trading is a round lot, which is 100 shares or a multiple thereof.

SECURITIES & EXCHANGE COMMISSION (SEC) – The federal agency that administers securities laws in the United

States. The SEC, created under the Securities Exchange Act of 1934, governs the following: registration of organized securities exchanges, proxy solicitation, disclosure requirements for securities in the secondary market and regulation of insider trading. This Act, along with the Securities Act of 1933, forms the basis of securities regulation.

SELL-TO-OPEN - The placing of an initial order by an option writer to sell an option in order to establish a position. The writer receives premium income from the buyer of the option. (Also referred to as "sell covered call.")

SHORT POSITION - An investment position where the investor has written an option with the contract obligation remaining outstanding.

SHORT-TERM - Relates to the gain or loss in a security that has been held for a certain period of time. For example, under current tax laws the gain or loss in a security held for less than one year would be short-term.

STRIKE PRICE - The price at which the holder (buyer) of a call option can purchase the underlying ETF. Also sometimes referred to as the "exercise price."

TICKER SYMBOL - The abbreviation for an ETF or option used on securities quotation machines. For example, "FFF" is the ETF ticker symbol for the Fortune 500 Index Tracking ETF and "FFFIO" is the option ticker symbol for FFF calls with a September expiration and a strike price of $75.

TIME VALUE - That part of an option's market price which is solely attributable to the remaining time before the expiration of the option. If the option is out-of-the-money or at-the-money, the entire premium is attributable to time value. If the option is in-the-money, the amount attributable to time value is calculated by subtracting the amount by which the option is in-the-money from the current option premium. For example, if the current market price of an option is $3 ½ and the option is in-the-money by $2, the time value is $1 ½.

UNCOVERED (NAKED) – Implies that the investor who writes a call option does not own the underlying ETF, so that if the ETF is assigned the writer must purchase shares at the current market price to deliver to the call holder (buyer). Also known as "naked" because, if the option is exercised, the writer is without shares and is caught naked. If the ETF subject to the call rises significantly, the writer could be exposed to substantial (theoretically unlimited) losses. This is an extremely high-risk strategy, even more speculative than buying calls.

UNDERLYING ETF - The ETF owned by the option writer that the option holder (buyer) has the right, but not the obligation, to purchase according to the terms of the option contract.

UNREALIZED GAIN – Occurs when the value of an unsold asset rises above its original cost. Also referred to as a "paper gain."

UNREALIZED LOSS – Occurs when the value of an unsold asset is reduced below its original cost. Also referred to as a "paper loss."

WRITING CALLS – Another term for selling covered call contracts on an ETF an investor owns.

The following support material has been added, which may be of little or considerable use to the ETF Investor, depending on personal experience with investing in general and the use of options in particular.

A GUIDE FOR
COVERED CALL OPTION WRITING

For investors who wish to use covered call option writing as an investment strategy, this guide will assure that all appropriate steps have been taken in the proper order:

STEP 1:

SELF-EDUCATION ON ETF SELECTION

The following books and Web sites are recommended for investors to be used as needed for educational purposes:

Beginning Investors: *The Wall Street Journal Guide To Understanding Money & Investing;* www.motleyfool.com

All Investors: *Beating The Street; The Exchange-Traded Funds Manual; Exchange Traded Funds: An Insider's Guide to Buying the Market;* www.marketwatch.com; www.cnbc.com; www.briefing.com

Seasoned Investors: *Stocks For The Long Run;* www.investors.com; www.wsj.com

STEP 2:

ESTABLISHING A BROKERAGE ACCOUNT

Due to lower commission costs, it is recommended that investors select a discount brokerage account and trade online or on the telephone using an automated voice response system. Fidelity and Charles Schwab are suggested for consideration due to their size, support capabilities and offerings of complete cash management accounts.

Action required: select and open account; obtain approval from brokerage to trade covered call options

Major discount brokers include:

Fidelity Investments: www.fidelity.com; 800-544-5555

Charles Schwab & Co.: www.schwab.com; 800-2-SCHWAB

Accutrade: www.accutrade.com; 800-494-8939

Ameritrade: www.ameritrade.com; 800-454-9272

CSFB Direct: www.csfbdirect.com; 800-825-5723

Datek: www.datek.com; 800-U2-DATEK

E-Trade: www.etrade.com; 800-ETRADE1

TD Waterhouse: www.tdwaterhouse.com; 800-TDWATERHOUSE

STEP 3:

ESTABLISH LIST OF PROSPECTIVE ETFs TO PURCHASE

For individual ETFs, select sufficient names that will assure adequate diversification to minimize risk. Maintain the list over time by researching these and other names so that an ongoing list of ETFs to fit the portfolio objectives is ready and current as cash becomes available for reinvestment. Use the brokerage account to be sure options are available for all ETFs on the list.

Utilize www.amex.com and www.nasdaq.com as a resource for determining what funds are available and to obtain prospectuses. Use your favorite search engine to find Web pages on "Exchange Traded Funds" or "ETF," which will provide links that may yield additional information.

STEP 4:

USE EXCEL TEMPLATE "CALLS" OR MANUAL WORKSHEET

Using the discount brokerage account, obtain and enter the required data onto the Excel "calls" worksheet or the manual worksheet for the Exchange Traded Funds in the above list to provide yield and other information. Select at least several examples of various expiration dates and strike prices for each.

STEP 5:

REVIEW "CALLS" WORKSHEET DATA AND MAKE OPTION WRITING SELECTIONS

Print out the "calls" worksheet and review the data or the manual worksheet data to make specific selections of option writing opportunities on your ETFs, giving consideration to call option diversification (expiration and strike price), and your overall targeted yield.

STEP 6:

INITIATE ETF TRADES
Initiate ETF purchase ("buy") trades with the discount broker based on final decisions as determined by the review. Verify that orders have been filled.

STEP 7:

INITIATE OPTION TRADES
Initiate call option writing ("sell-to-open," also known as "sell covered call") trades with the discount broker based on final decisions as determined by the review. Verify that orders have been filled. Consider how to use the premium income deposited into your account the next day after trades are filled.

STEP 8:

USE EXCEL TEMPLATE "RESULTS" OR MANUAL WORKSHEET
From the discount brokerage account confirmations (either hard copy or online), enter the required data onto the Excel "results" worksheet (use the "Trade Sort" tab) or the manual worksheet as a permanent record of covered call writing trades. Copy and paste this data into other tabs on the worksheet and sort, as desired.

STEP 9:

FOR ETFS SOLD THROUGH ASSIGNMENT OF CALLS AT EXPIRATION

Go back to Step 4 and select new ETFs when cash is received from sales of an ETF due to assignment of call options, or if ETFs are sold for any other reason. Continue forward through the rest of the steps.

STEP 10:

FOR COVERED CALL OPTIONS THAT EXPIRE AND ARE NOT EXERCISED (ETF IS NOT ASSIGNED)

Go back to Step 5 and enter data for ETFs when calls expire unexercised. Continue forward through the rest of the steps.

HOW TO DETERMINE
THE SYMBOL FOR AN OPTION

The single best and fastest way to determine an option symbol is to look up the "option chain" for an ETF through an online discount brokerage account (see Chapter 9 for details). You may also call your broker for the information. An option symbol may, however, be determined manually in many, but not all, cases.

Every option has a symbol assigned to it, just as every ETF has a ticker symbol. An investor needs to know what the symbol is for an option in order to look up its latest price, bid and ask, volume of trades and other information, as well as to trade the option contract. The information given below will assist the option investor in determining the symbol for many, but not all, call options.

The option symbol consists of three components:

The ticker symbol for the underlying ETF (or in the case of LEAPS and in some other cases, a substitute for it)

A letter indicating the month in which the option expires, and

A letter indicating the strike price of the option

Ticker Symbol – All call options on ETFs begin with a three-letter symbol for the ETF, although not always the same three letters. For example, the QQQ call for expiration in March, 2003 at a strike price of $35 begins with "QQQ," the same symbol as the ETF. The call option expiring in March, 2003 with a strike price of $33, however, begins with the letters "QAV." The January, 2003 $70 call begins with "QUE" and the January, 2003 $75 call begins with "YQQ." There would be no way for the investor to know this without checking with a broker, either directly or online. Again, there are never more than five letters in an option symbol. Since the next to the last letter signifies the expiration and the last letter indicates the strike price, there is room for no more than three additional letters at the beginning. If this is confusing to you, welcome to the club.

CALL OPTION EXPIRATION DATES AND STRIKE PRICES

Expiration Letter – The next to the last letter in the option symbol signifies the expiration of the option according to the following schedule:

MONTH	LETTER
January	A
February	B
March	C
April	D

May	E
June	F
July	G
August	H
September	I
October	J
November	K
December	L

Strike Price Letter – The last letter in the option symbol signifies the strike price of the option according to the following schedule:

STRIKE PRICE	LETTER	STRIKE PRICE	LETTER
$5	A	$70	N
$10	B	$75	O
$15	C	$80	P
$20	D	$85	Q
$25	E	$90	R
$30	F	$95	S
$35	G	$00	T
$40	H	$7 ½	U
$45	I	$12 ½	V
$50	J	$17 ½	W
$55	K	$22 ½	X
$60	L	$27 ½	Y
$65	M	$32 ½	Z

Thus, for the Fortune 500 Index Fund (ETF symbol "FFF") October $70 calls, the option symbol is FFFJN ("FFF" is for the ETF symbol, "J" is for the April calls, and "N" is for the $70 strike price.

The Vanguard Total ETF Market Vipers (ETF symbol "VTI") December $100 calls would have the symbol VTILT ("VTI" is for the ETF symbol, "L" is for the September calls, and "T" is for the $100 strike price). Note that the symbol "T" would apply whether the price of an ETF is $100, $200, $300, and so on.

On rare occasions you may find an ETF which has a $37 ½, $42 ½, $47 ½ or higher option contract available. As all of the letters of the alphabet are used for strike prices from $5 through $32 ½, these higher strike prices also use a letter that is used for another strike price. This can be confusing, and your broker should be contacted to be sure you have the proper symbol.

FINDING QUOTES FOR OPTIONS
WITH NO ONLINE BROKERAGE ACCOUNT

Many daily newspapers and financial newspapers provide option quotes, however, they are incomplete. *The Wall Street Journal, Barron's* and *Investors Business Daily* each provide a limited number of closing quotes on some of the more actively traded options each day.

For those who have online access (many local libraries have computers and Internet connections if needed), a very broad array of option quotes can be obtained at no cost (with only twenty-minute delay from real-time) through the Yahoo! Web site, www.yahoo.com.   After entering the

Yahoo! Web site, click on "Finance." Then enter the ETF ticker symbol for the underlying ETF on which you wish to write options (e.g., FFF for Fortune 500 Index Fund). On the box just to the right, click on the menu arrow and select "Options," then click on "Get." The next window displays choices for calls on the left-hand side of the page. Above the "Calls" box, click on the expiration date for calls on which you wish to obtain quotes. A table of quotes appears on call options available for the expiration date you have selected. The following information is displayed: option symbol, last trade, change, bid, ask, volume, open interest, and strike price. Even more information is available by clicking on any option symbol.

HOW TO USE THE MICROSOFT® EXCEL TEMPLATE "CALLS" TO CALCULATE COVERED CALL WRITING OPPORTUNITIES

The Excel template provided on the 3 ½" floppy diskette with this book is designed to make covered call writing calculations as simple as possible. Microsoft® Excel is needed to run this template. The template provided can only be used on a PC unless Mac users have file-sharing software.

Follow these instructions to use the template:

Place the diskette into your floppy drive. Start your Excel program and load the template (the file is named "calls") from your "A" drive.

You may wish to save the template on your hard drive and may do so by clicking on the word "File" in the upper left hand corner of the worksheet and then clicking on "Save As" when the menu drops down. In the "File name" type "calls," which will save it under the same file name as on the floppy diskette.

Completing the worksheet:

Note that on the template there are groupings of three lines for each ETF. You probably won't need more than three lines for each ETF on which you are seeking option writing opportunities. However, if you do, simply insert additional rows at the end of a set and copy more of the lines as needed (see your Excel program manual for details if you don't know how to do this).

In cell C1 is the formula "=today()." Do not change this, as this is needed to automatically calculate the number of days in column H.

You will see an "x" under some columns in row 2. This means that you need to supply information into these columns to complete the template.

Complete as follows:

Column A: Enter the ETF ticker symbol for the ETF.

Column B: Enter the number of shares you own or are contemplating buying.

Column C: Enter the current price per share or your cost of the ETF, which ever is the most meaningful to you to compute your yield. If you have owned the ETF for a long time and it is worth more than you paid for it, you may wish to use the market value rather than your cost basis, as that will give you a more accurate yield based on current value.

Column E: Enter the dividend per share, if any, the ETF currently pays (note: this is not always readily obtained information).

Column F: You will note that starting in cell number U6 there are numerous expiration dates. Enter the expiration date of the option under consideration by clicking on the appropriate date. Then click the "Copy" button, move the cursor to the appropriate cell in column F and click, then click the "Paste" button. The expiration date you desire will be transferred. Note: with the passage of time, you can add additional expiration dates at the bottom of the list and delete ones that expire. Simply type in the appropriate expiration date for future use. Use the third Friday of the month for expiration dates. If the expiration date is February 15, 2004 you should type 2/15/2004.

Column G: Enter the strike price of the option.

Column I: Enter the option symbol for the option under consideration (note: see "How To Determine the Symbol for an Option" in this Appendix, obtain symbols from option chain data if you have an online brokerage account or by phoning your broker).

Column J: Enter the current price of the premium (this should be approximately the average between the current bid and ask prices, or perhaps a little less).

After entering this information, the rest of the data will be completed by the template for your review.

The template is currently configured so that no brokerage commissions are included in the calculations. If you would like to customize the template to factor in brokerage commissions on your option trade and ETF trade calculations (when the ETF is called away from you at expiration), it can be done very easily using your commission schedule.

Place your cursor in cell S4 on the Excel template. Typically commissions on option trades are charged at a flat dollar amount and then a certain dollar amount per contract traded. Enter the flat dollar amount that applies to your schedule in cell S4. Then enter the dollar amount per contract charge in cell S5. Finally, the assumption is made that you are trading through an online discount brokerage account. If that is the case, you are most likely paying a flat rate on your ETF trades at least up to 1,000 shares. Enter the flat dollar amount of commission you are paying on your ETF trades in cell T4.

If your commission schedule is figured on a different basis than that described here, simply convert it to approximate the above schedule. It is not critically important that the brokerage commissions be exact. It is a reasonably small factor in your return calculations. You may choose to ignore commissions entirely in your calculations, or try to get it as exact as possible. The choice is yours.

HOW TO USE A DISCOUNT BROKER WITHOUT A COMPUTER AND CALCULCATING COVERED CALL WRITING OPPORTUNITIES MANUALLY

If you do not access your discount broker online, everything in this book is still available to you. Instead of obtaining quotes and executing your trades online, you will need to do this by telephone...either through direct conversation with a representative of your discount brokerage or by using their automated service whereby you press numbers on your touch-tone phone. It is recommended that you use the automated voice response phone system rather than speaking with a representative when initiating trades, as commissions can be significantly lower. Be sure that the discount broker you are using or considering offers the touch-tone automated phone access.

You should request instructions from your broker on how to use their service, as brokerages operate their systems somewhat differently. You may wish to utilize a representative personally at first until you become more comfortable with using the automated voice response phone system. All quotes and trading capabilities that are offered through a discount broker's Web site are offered through their representatives and are typically offered through their touch-tone automated voice response phone system as well. Therefore, while this may be a bit more laborious than obtaining quotes and trading online, you have access to everything you need to carry out the strategies in this book.

Complete the manual calculation page as described below. Sheets are included at the end of the book and may be removed and copied. By following these instructions, you can make the same accurate calculations that are made using the Excel template...but this way is more work.

Column (A): Enter the name of the ETF you own.
Column (B): Enter the ticker symbol for the ETF.
Column (C): Enter the number of shares you own or are contemplating buying.
Column (D): Enter the current price per share.
Column (E): Multiply Column (C) and Column (D).
Column (F): Enter the dividend per share the ETF currently pays.
Column (G): Enter the expiration date of the option under consideration.
Column (H): Enter the strike price of the option.
Column (I): Enter the number of days between today's date and the expiration date.
Column (J): Enter the option symbol for the option under consideration (note: see "How to Determine the Symbol for an Option" under this Appendix).
Column (K): Enter the current price for the premium (this should be approximately the average between the current bid and ask prices, or perhaps a little less).
Column (L): Multiply Column (C) by Column (K) (reduce the total by the projected commission cost if complete accuracy is desired in the calculations).
Column (M): Divide Column (L) by Column (I).

Column (N): Divide Column (L) by Column (E).
Column (O): Multiply Column (N) by 365/Column (I).
Then, if the ETF pays a dividend, divide Column (F) by
Column (D) and add the result to the previous calculation.
Column (P): Subtract Column (D) from Column (H)
and multiply the difference by Column (C) (reduce the total
by the projected commission cost to sell the ETF if complete
accuracy is desired in the calculations).
Column (Q): Divide Column (P) by Column (E). Then
multiply that result by 365/Column I. Then add that result
to Column (O).

If you are placing your order with a live representative
at your brokerage, it is important that you say the right
things for the sake of efficiency and to be sure that you are
stating the information correctly so no mistakes are made
either by you or by your broker. Phone calls are typically
recorded.

Let's say that you have 1,000 shares of QQQ on which
you wish to write calls. After analyzing your alternatives,
you have decided to write ten contracts (remember, one call
contract equals 100 shares) of the January 2003 calls with a
strike price of $25. The price you would like to get is $2.00
per contract, so you will be placing a limit order. (You could
place a market order, however, placing limit orders is
usually recommended due to the wide spreads that often
occur between bid and ask prices on options.) You can
either specify "good for the day" or "good 'til canceled," as
you prefer.

To place the above order you would say to your broker's representative something like, "I would like to sell-to-open ten contracts of the QQQ January, 2003 $25 calls at a limit price of $2.00, good for the day."

HOW TO USE THE MICROSOFT® EXCEL TEMPLATE "RESULTS" TO TRACK YOUR OPTION WRITING TRANSACTIONS

The Excel template provided on the 3 ½" floppy diskette with this book is designed to make tracking of your covered call option writing program results as simple as possible. Microsoft® Excel is needed to run this template. The template provided can only be used on a PC unless Mac users have file-sharing software.

Follow these instructions to use the template:

1. Place the diskette into your floppy drive. Start your Excel program and load the template (the file is named "results") from your "A" drive.

2. You may wish to save the template on your hard drive and may do so by clicking on the word "File" in the upper left hand corner of the worksheet and then clicking on "Save As" when the menu drops down. In the "File name" type "results," which will save it under the same file name as on the floppy diskette.

3. Completing the worksheet:

You should begin by being sure that you are working with the "TRADE SORT" tab of the template, which is located in the lower left hand corner of the worksheet, as the data in this worksheet is used as input for the other tabs.

You will see an "x" under some columns in row 3. This means that you need to supply information into these columns to make the template work. New rows can be added by replicating the information into the appropriate cells.

Complete as follows:

Column A: Enter an abbreviation for the account type for this option transaction (i.e. you may wish to use "PERS" for a personal taxable account and "IRA" for an IRA account. Use whatever abbreviations are meaningful for you, as long as you are consistent.)

Column B: Enter the ETF ticker symbol for the ETF.

Column C: Enter the number of shares on which options were written for this transaction.

Column D: Enter the price per share at the time the option transaction was initiated or your cost of the ETF, which ever is the most meaningful to you, to compute your yield. If you have owned the ETF for a long time and it is worth more than you paid for it, you may wish to use the market value rather than your cost basis, as that will give you a more accurate yield based on current value.

Column F: Enter the date that the option transaction took place (for example, if the date of the transaction was August 15, 2002 you should type in 8/15/2002.

Column G: You will note that starting in cell number P6 there are numerous expiration dates. Enter the expiration date for the option transaction by positioning the cursor on the appropriate expiration date in column P. Then click the "Copy" button, move the cursor to the appropriate cell in column G and click, then click the "Paste" button. The expiration date you desire will be transferred. Note: with the passage of time, you can add additional expiration dates at the bottom of the list and delete ones that expire. Simply type in the appropriate expiration date for future use. Use the third Friday of the month for expiration dates. You can also simply type in the expiration date. If the expiration date is February 15, 2003 you should type in 2/15/2003.

Column H: Enter the strike price of the option.

Column J: Enter the option symbol for the option transaction.

Column K: Enter the price of the premium per contract received for the option transaction.

Column L: Enter the exact amount of premium income received as stated on the brokerage confirmation report for this option transaction. Note: If the options are bought to close prior to expiration, reduce the amount of the premium income received for this transaction by the cost to purchase the contracts as stated on the brokerage confirmation report.

Column M: If the underlying shares are assigned upon expiration, enter the total of any capital appreciation or depreciation in this column, either using your cost basis or the market value of the ETF at the time the option transaction was initiated, as you deem appropriate.

After entering this information, the rest of the data will be completed by the template.

4. Completing the other tabs on the worksheet:

If you desire, the information from the "Trade Sort" tab can be copied and pasted into one or more of the other tabs to view the information in different ways. The "Expiration Sort" tab will allow you to see the same information sorted by expiration date. The "ETF Sort" tab sorts the information by ETF, regardless of which account it may be in. The "Account Sort" tab sorts the information by account.

Start by going to the "Trade Sort" template and highlight all of the data by placing the cursor in the upper left hand cell where your data starts.

Press down on your mouse button and drag the cursor to the right and down until it darkens all of the data cells on your worksheet.

Then let go of the mouse button and all of your data will be selected.

Now click on the "Copy" icon at the top and click on the tab at the bottom you wish to use. It will take you to that worksheet, which appears the same as the worksheet for "Trade Sort."

Point and click the cursor into the same cell address as the cell from which you copied the data. Then all you have to do is click on the "Paste" icon and all of the data you copied will be pasted into the new worksheet.

Each of the tabbed worksheets has been formatted so that they will sort according to what the tab says. All you need to do now is click on the word "Data" at the top. A drop down menu box will appear. Click on "Sort" and another drop down menu comes up. Just click on the "OK" box at the bottom and your data is sorted.

HOW TO TRACK YOUR OPTION WRITING TRANSACTIONS MANUALLY

Complete the manual calculation page as described below. Sheets are included at the end of the book and may be removed and copied. By following these instructions, you can develop the same transaction records that are created by using the Excel template...but this way is more work.

Column (A): Enter the name of the ETF you own.

Column (B): Enter the ticker symbol for the ETF.

Column (C): Enter the number of shares on which you have written options for this transaction.

Column (D): Enter the current price per share.

Column (E): Multiply Column (C) and Column (D).

Column (F): Enter the trade date of the option transaction.

Column (G): Enter the expiration date of the option.

Column (H): Enter the strike price of the option.

Column (I): Enter the number of days between the option transaction date and the expiration date.

Column (J): Enter the option symbol for the option written.

Column (K): Enter the premium price per contract for this transaction.

Column (L): Enter the total net premium income received from the
brokerage confirmation report.

Column (M): If the underlying ETF is called away at expiration of the option, enter the total amount of gain or loss on the ETF based upon the cost basis of the ETF or the market value at the time the option was written, which ever you deem appropriate.

Column (N): Add Column (L) and Column (M).

Column (O): Divide Column (N) by Column (E) and multiply that figure by 365 divided by Column (I).

SUGGESTED READING

The following books are suggested as possible readings for individuals desiring to learn more about market basics, how markets work and Exchange Traded Funds:

THE WALL STREET JOURNAL GUIDE TO UNDER-STANDING MONEY & INVESTING by Kenneth M. Morris, Virginia B. Morris, Alan M. Siegel, August 1999, paperback, 160 pages. This handy fact-filled book initiates you into the mysteries of the financial pages...buying ETFs, bonds, mutual funds, futures and options, spotting trends and evaluating companies. A good beginning level investment book. Currently available over the Internet through Amazon.com for $12.76.

ONLINE INVESTING: The Wall Street Journal Interactive Edition's Complete Guide to Becoming A Successful Internet Investor by Dave Pettit (Contributor), Rich Jaroslovsky, 1st edition, May 23, 2000, hardback, 342 pages. The editors of the online version of *The Wall Street Journal* have produced a comprehensive overview of the best Web sites and resources available to the online investor. It tells where to find the best interactive tools, online calculators, and worksheets for selecting ETFs and mutual funds and for researching and charting investments. Many other financial topics are covered. Currently available over the Internet through Amazon.com for $20.00.

THE EXCHANGE-TRADED FUNDS MANUAL by Gary Gastineau, February 2002, hardcover, 401 pages. This is a comprehensive book on every aspect of Exchange Traded Funds. If you have any questions about ETFs, they will likely be answered by this book. Currently available over the Internet through Amazon.com for $41.97.

EXCHANGE TRADED FUNDS: An Insider's Guide to Buying the Market by Jim Wiant, Will McClatchy, Nathan Most, Indexfunds.com, November, 2001; hardcover, 288 pages. This book provides essential background on the rapid proliferation of ETFs worldwide, specific product information, and a range of useful investment applications for different types of investors, all in a highly readable framework. The book dispels the myths associated with this popular new index product. Currently available over the Internet through Amazon.com for $20.97.

Note: Books are available in used condition from time to time through Amazon.com at significantly reduced prices.

```
┌─────────────────────────────────┐
│                                 │
│   BROKERAGE & ETF WEB           │
│   SITES ON THE INTERNET         │
│                                 │
└─────────────────────────────────┘
```

The following Web sites may be useful to those desiring basic information about options, discount brokerages and ETFs.

OPTIONS

www.cboe.com – Chicago Board Options Exchange. This is the largest exchange for trading options. The CBOE Web site is a tremendously valuable resource about how options work. This is probably the best educational site about options available to the nonprofessional. The booklet *Characteristics and Risks of Standardized Options* is available on this Web site.

DISCOUNT BROKERAGES

All of the following provide quotes on various securities and online investment capabilities for ETFs, options, Exchange Traded Funds, bonds, mutual funds, and other types of investments. Some provide general business news, company specific news, investment research, and other information. This list is not meant to be exhaustive, but is representative of the largest online discount brokers. Information on these and other companies is available at libraries for non-computer users.

www.fidelity.com - Fidelity Investments; 800-544-5555

www.schwab.com - Charles Schwab & Co.; 800-2-SCHWAB

www.accutrade.com - Accutrade; 800-494-8939

www.ameritrade.com - Ameritrade; 800-454-9272

www.csfbdirect.com - CSFB Direct; 800-825-5723

www.datek.com - Datek; 800-U2-DATEK

www.etrade.com - E-Trade; 800-ETRADE1

www.tdwaterhouse.com - TD Waterhouse; 800-TDWATERHOUSE

EXCHANGE TRADED FUNDS

www.amex.com – Web site of the American Stock Exchange. Among other things, the site contains a list of all Exchange Traded Funds.

www.ft.com – News stories and other information from the Financial Times.

www.nasdaq.com – Web site of the NASDAQ stock market. For information about ETFs click on "Investment Products," then "Exchange Traded Funds."

www.ishares.com – Information on ETFs offered by Barclays Global Investors.

www.ldrs.com – Information on ETFs offered by Merrill Lynch.

INDEX

wsj.com, 132
Wall Street Journal Guide To
  Understanding Money &
  Investing, 132, 151

writing calls, 130

Yahoo! Finance, 27, 99, 139

ABOUT THE AUTHOR

 As a thirty-year career banker and trust officer for Norwest Corporation, now Wells Fargo & Co., one of the nation's largest financial institutions, Paul D. Kadavy was president of numerous banks in three states. He also headed a multi-billion dollar trust department, managed a team of investment professionals, and was a trusted advisor to many of the banks' individual clients. He is now retired from banking and is a writer, teacher and public speaker.

Kadavy is a faculty member of several community colleges in the Phoenix Metropolitan area and has served on the faculty of the National Graduate Trust School at Northwestern University, The Schools of Banking, Inc. and the American Institute of Banking. He has been a lecturer on trust, investment and banking subjects to FDIC and Federal Reserve Bank examiners in Washington, D.C. He has been a public speaker for the past twenty-five years.

Kadavy is also the author of *Covered Call Writing Demystified* and *The Book of World-Class Quotations: The Best of the Best Quotations on Earth*, which includes guides for writing affirmations and for personal goal setting. All of his books are available through Arrow Publications and Amazon.com. In addition to writing books, he is the author of banking, trust and investment articles for such national publications as *Financial Review*, *Trusts & Estates*, *Pension World*, *The Collector/Investor*, *Cases & Comment* and *American Bankers Association Trust Management*.

He has developed and successfully used the principles in his presentations and this book for almost twenty years.